Focus on SHANGHAI

HONG KONG CHINA TOURISM PRESS

Preface

Located on the coast of the East China Sea, Shanghai is the largest city in China. With convenient transport by land, sea and air, it is both a tourist base in China's southeastern coastal area and a tourist site for visitors from home and abroad.

In terms of landscape, Shanghai has neither famous mountains, large rivers, exotic peaks or vales, nor world-famous historical sites. Nevertheless it is a magnet to tourists from everywhere.

Shanghai is, so to say, a window of China. Some foreign tourists believe that to trace China's history of 2,000 years, one goes to Xi'an, the capital of Shaanxi Province; to see her 1,000-year-old civilization, Beijing is the city to visit; and to examine China's history of the past century, Shanghai is the best place. This view has become the sustaining image of the city.

Being a historic city, Shanghai sports hundreds of buildings in different shapes and styles that are both modern and Occidental. They are not only the testimony of the city's vicissitudes over the past century, but also evidence of its fame as "an international architectural exhibition". Shanghai is, like other metropolises in the world, a shopping paradise, with crowds of eager shoppers surging day and night along Nanjing Road and Huaihai Road, the two major commercial streets in the city.

The Bund is the landmark of Shanghai, never missed by visitors to the city. The most well-known sightseeing spots — Waibaidu Bridge and the long embankment along the Huangpu River — and scores of different styles of Western buildings concentrate in this area. And the rapid changes of the Bund in recent years also symbolize the new look of the whole city.

Moreover, the construction of the world-class Nanpu and Yangpu bridges, that link the eastern part with the western part of the city, has made Shanghai people's 700-year dream a reality. Apart from their practical value, the two bridges have become the city's newest tourist attractions.

Picturesque parks and gardens, numbering several scores, and the famous monasteries, international Christian and Catholic churches as well as mosques in the city are also ideal tourist spots. Convenient and with a wealth of choice, visitors can find restaurants, cafes, bars and amusement facilities everywhere in this flourishing city.

This special book will serve you as a guide, bringing you to discover the metropolis of Shanghai.

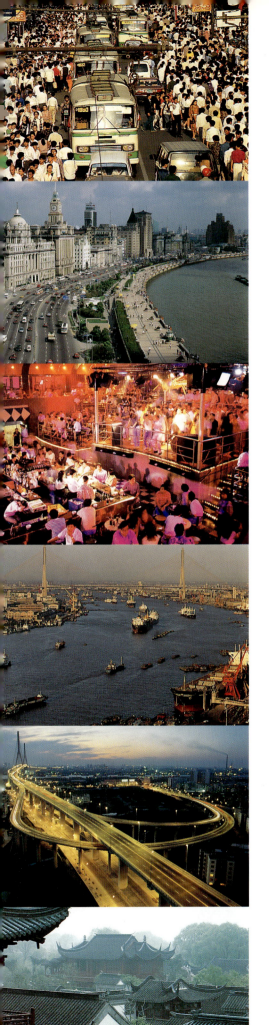

Contents

Preface	2
The New Look of "Big Shanghai"	4
Shanghai's Architectural Potpourri	18
Shanghai's Kaleidoscopic Changes	28
The New Bund — Where Gold Flows and Colours Sparkle	40
A Natural Barrier Has Turned into a Thoroughfare?	50
A Glimpse of Pudong	54
Night in Shanghai	58
A Paradise for Collectors	66
Visiting Ancient Songjiang County Town	72
Festival of the Virgin Mary at Sheshan	76
A Garden in the Land of Water	82
Tourist Guide to Shanghai	88

The New Look of "Big Shanghai"

TEXT BY CHAN YAT NIN

A Bird's-Eye View of "Big Shanghai"

As of October 1994, people can have a bird's-eye view of Shanghai from this height of over 400 metres, which is the tallest structure in Asia. From this height, one has to admit that the earth-shaking changes in the 1990s that are taking place in Shanghai are creating a miracle (by Xie Guanghui).

Shanghai, the largest city in China, has a population of more than 10 million and the most economic power among all cities and provinces on China's mainland. Such factors like these have crowned the city with the "big", thus the city is better known as the "Big Shanghai".

Though Shanghai played the most important role in the changes that took place in China in the past few decades, the city itself, however, had more or less remained the same. Then changes in Shanghai in the past three years suddenly took everybody by surprise. Compared with its history of becoming a small town only in the last century and growing into a prosperous metropolis with the reputation of being "Paris in the Orient" early this century, what has just happened is a much more impressive miracle.

Once a financial centre in the Far East, Shanghai has again emerged as a flagship in the waves of reform and opening up when the centre of economic development in China shifted eastward in the last few years. In the age of fundamental changes in Shanghai, there is the revival of century-old customs blended with Chinese and foreign cultural traditions, the steady emergence of new and trendy life styles, the straight progress of modern finance and economics in this most urban and most densely populated city of China, the Shanghai people with their unique qualities and characteristics once again feeling in their element during a new height of economic development.... All this constitutes the new look of the "Big Shanghai" today.

Pearl of the Orient
Shanghai is also known as the "Pearl of the Orient". Now people in Shanghai have built the Asia's tallest TV tower, rightly called the "Pearl of the Orient". Cast in the festival lights, it seems all the more an attractive and bright pearl (by Xie Guanghui).

The Bund at Festival
The Bund during festivals is all the more a symbol of Shanghai. Local residents, visitors from other cities and towns and foreigners all converge here, packing the road and enjoying themselves to their hearts' content (by Xie Guanghui).

The Pudong Area

The Huangpu River cuts Shanghai into two halves. On the west bank has always been the prosperous metropolis while on the east was once a poor rural area. Then all of a sudden, Pudong (East of the Huangpu River) became the forefront of development as high-rises began to grow in the rice fields and vegetable gardens. Lujiazui, which looks at the Bund in downtown Shanghai across the river, is progressing quickly towards the goal of becoming a modern financial and trade centre, or simply a new Bund, and a new Shanghai (by Lu Yun).

No. 1 Commercial Street in China

Facing page top:
The sparkling neon lights on the Nanjing Road at night are also something unsurpassed anywhere in China (by Chan Yat Nin).

Facing page bottom:
One look at the floods of pedestrians on the Nanjing Road will make any businessman's heart beat fast with excitement — why not get hold of a spot on the street and open a business? (by Xie Guanghui)

Nanjing Road, known as the "No. 1 Commercial Street in China", is a heaven for shoppers (by Xie Guanghui).

The Yangpu Bridge

No bridges on the Huangpu River? That's history already. During the 1990s, two world-class bridges spanned the river. The Yangpu Bridge which was built after the Nanpu Bridge is the largest cable-braced bridge in the world (by Lu Yun).

Once the Shanghai Racing Court opened by foreigners in Shanghai, the place was turned in the early 1950s into the People's Square, where large mass gatherings used to be held. The 1990s is seeing a major facelift of the square. With the Civic Centre completed, the municipal government moved its offices from the commercial area along the Bund to this spot which has become a symbol of Shanghai's plan of "fundamental changes in three years" (by Xie Guanghui).

In the centre of the People's Square, the round-shaped Shanghai Museum stands on an elevated square foundation. This design symbolizes the old saying that the heaven is round and the earth square. The idea is to combine modernity with a tone of history (by Xie Guanghui).

The People's Square

The fountain in the People's Square, just like pearls falling into a jade plate, draws residents over to enjoy a stroll by its side (by Xie Guanghui).

A New Nighttown
The economic development zones are changing the face of the great metropolis as new towns rise in Pudong, Hongqiao, Minhang, Caohejing, Gubei and other districts. The Hongqiao Economic & Technological Development Zone is just one of the nighttowns (by Lu Yun).

The magnificent architecture on the Bund in Shanghai (by Lu Yun)

Shanghai's Architectural Potpourri

PHOTOS BY CHAN YAT NIN
ARTICLE BY ER DONGQIANG

From the top of Shanghai Mansions, built in 1934, at the northern end of the Bund I looked out over buildings revealing a hotchpotch of architectural origins. Built mainly between the turn of the century and the 1930s by the British, the French, the Americans and citizens of sundry other countries, they have earned Shanghai the Chinese nickname "Exhibition of World Architecture".

The foreign presence dates from 1842 and the "unequal treaty", the Treaty of Nanjing, under which China was forced to open five ports to international trade following her defeat in the Opium War. Before that date Shanghai was a small but prosperous walled city and anchorage for fishing and trading vessels. By a series of Land Regulations, foreign enclaves were leased along the waterfront. In 1863 the British and American enclaves were amalgamated into what became known as the International Settlement, separated from the French Concession, established in 1849, by a creek which is now the line of Yan'an Road. By 1920, according to the census of that year, the population had grown to almost one million, including 26,800 foreigners from a rich mix of nationalities. Shanghai was for all practical purposes a neutral and self-governing entity not subject to the authority of the Qing government in Beijing. Apart from the hundreds of thousands of hardworking local people who flocked to participate in the commercial and industrial boom at all levels, it also proved a magnet for fortune-hunters, smugglers, rebels and conspirators. Its flamboyant lifestyle was proverbial in the West and drew the wrath of many foreign missionaries. Modern in outlook, in the 1930s Shanghai had the tallest buildings and the most motor vehicles of any city in Asia.

The city of Shanghai today still contains over 300 office buildings, private houses and religious edifices with a foreign flavour. If we were to review them one by one, it would take us forever and it would be difficult to know just where to begin. So why don't we start right here, with the sights of the Bund? The Bund (an Anglo-Indian word meaning "embankment") extends south along the western bank of the River Huangpu from its confluence with Suzhou Creek to the vicinity of Fuzhou Road. It is now called Zhongshan Road East. A string of handsome edifices in sundry styles, originally erected as embassies, hotels, exclusive clubs, company premises, agencies and banks, line the Bund on the side away from the river. Most of them, consisting of a single compact structure, are adorned with clock towers and turrets, colonnades, marble pillars, wrought-iron entrances and other examples of ornamental architecture with the result that each presents a distinctively individual appearance. Whether viewed from a distance or admired close up, these buildings have a special charm all their own.

Take the building which is now the seat of the People's Municipal Government, for instance. This seven-storey edifice, completed in 1921, was formerly the premises of the Hongkong and Shanghai Bank. It has a foundation of massive, unpolished granite, firm and solid, the very embodiment of what one would hope for in a reliable bank. It is of majestic proportions, with an Ionic colonnade on its facade. It is topped with a splendid dome. The Shanghai Foreign Trade Bureau (formerly the British Consulate) is Victorian in style; it replaced an earlier structure which burnt down in 1870. The Customs House is a classical building with a fine neo-Grecian metalwork portico. At the intersection between Zhongshan Road East and Nanjing Road, the blue pyramid which crowns the north building of the Peace Hotel is most eye-catching.

The two buildings which together make up the hotel were built about 20 years apart and in different styles. The southern building, the former Palace Hotel, dates from 1904. Its proportions are classical with an emphasis on symmetry, as is evident from the arrangement of the windows. The north building, on the other hand, once the Cathay Hotel, was constructed in 1928 according to the neo-Classical bias of the Chicago School. This was the creation of Ellice Victor Sassoon of the famous Sassoon family, Jewish merchants from Baghdad by way of Bombay.

With the approach of dusk, the din of the traffic on the Bund gradually died down. The chimes from the clock tower on top of the Customs House were clearly audible. As the echoes faded into the distance and the contours of the imposing buildings stood out clearly against the darkening sky, our thoughts were inevitably drawn back to ponder on Shanghai's special "international" status in the early 20 th century....

Further south, at Guangdong Road, our eyes were drawn to the soft light radiating from a stained-glass window. Set in a house more or less the same as others of foreign style on the Bund, the intricately coloured and patterned glass lifted it out from the usual moulds. But as it was almost dark, we put off taking a good look at this intriguing building until the following day.

When we returned next morning, we discovered that the mansion is now a sort of billiards and video games centre. The moment we stepped inside, we noted the vaulted ceiling covered with glittering mosaics in Byzantine style, portraying daintily tripping maidens in Hellenic dress against a golden background, also in mosaic. More beautiful mosaic patterns with cherubs adorned the tops of the marble pillars which support the ceiling. Several groups of marble angels were sculpted in the spaces between the pillars. If it were not for the red Chinese lanterns suspended from the ceiling, one might well imagine oneself to be in some great villa in southern Europe.

This three-storey mansion has a long, narrow window at each staircase landing overlooking the street. They too are of stained

1. The "golden cage" on Guangdong Road boasts marvellous stained-glass windows.
2. Ceilings with a Byzantine flavour

glass with meticulous patterns, completely Western in theme and execution, symbolizing such virtues as prudence and fortitude. The sunlight pouring in highlighted the brilliancy of the colours. We lingered in the house for quite some time before we found somebody who knew anything about its history. He told us that this was the notorious "golden cage" in which the colourful character Yu Aqing used to keep his concubines.

Next we turned our attention to Nanjing Road, described in the past as the "ten-*li* foreign market", Shanghai's busiest commercial district for over a century. According to the article "Miscellaneous Notes on a Shanghai Tour" written in 1876 by Ge Yuanxu, a Hangzhou gentleman who lived in Shanghai for 50 years, Nanjing Road used to be a sundry goods centre. There used to be dealers specializing in Chinese silks and embroidery, imported cloth and woollens, Chinese musical instruments and other imported items such as musical boxes, microscopes, clocks, watches and thermometers. Fashionable late-Qing men of letters used to ride around in horse-drawn cabs and patronize the foreign shops on Nanjing Road. Later this was the location of the Wing On and Sincere department stores.

There are several other streets running east and west parallel to Nanjing Road which intersect with Zhongshan Road East. They too contain buildings in a variety of Western styles, although they are not quite as imposing as those on the former Bund. When the sun shines obliquely into these streets, catching the rough granite walls of the houses and burnishing them with its warmth, it is no wonder that European tourists love to linger in these streets, feeling quite at home, while savouring something of Shanghai's not so distant past.

While the Bund in the early 20th century was the heart of the International Settlement, the centre of international finance and capital, most of the owners of the foreign banks, as well as ranking Chinese officials and the Chinese aristocracy, lived in the residential quarters in the western part of the city, now the districts of Jing'an, Luwan and Xuhui.

We decided to visit Jing'an District first, walking straight down Nanjing Road to reach it. Once in the general area, we went to the top of the City Hotel for a bird's-eye view. My companion pointed out an unusual-looking building right under our noses. He told me this now contained the offices of the Shanghai Municipal Committee of the Youth League. This large building is irregular in shape, jutting out here and turning in there, haphazardly, the roof incorporating many turrets of different heights covered with glazed tiles. Part of the roof even incorporated pieces of coloured glass. Though it is said to have been based on a Norwegian design, this building has also

1. *The supposedly Norwegian-style Moller residence*
2. *Another mansion looks like a miniature castle.*
3. *The Customs House on the Bund has a bronze portal (by Gong Jianhua).*
4. *A large garden in front of Moller residence*

the dogs and horses which had started him on his upward path, Moller had them buried in graves dug in the garden of his home.

The Moller residence, however, is not the only one in the Jing'an District which comes

*1. Central European flavour of apartment blocks in Jing'an District
2. Beautifully maintained, the airy French grace of what is now the Art and Crafts Research Institute.
3. Houses with Western-style chimneys in the same district
4. Embellishing the goldfish pond at the Shanghai Federation of Literary and Art Circle's garden on Julu Road: a sumptuous maiden and four water babies.
5. The Russian-influenced Exhibition Hall occupies the site of Hardoon's garden.*

evidently absorbed the styles of other countries. We learned that altogether there are 106 rooms, large and small, and that its walls, floors, ceilings, stairs and cellars are all unconventional.

This building was in fact a house originally belonging to a merchant by the name of Eric Moller, and all the rooms in it had been laid out according to what his daughter had seen in her dreams. An adventurer (old Shanghai was known as a "paradise for adventurers"), Moller had come to the city penniless and made a fortune through dog and horse-racing and speculation. He was thus able to raise enough money to set up a ship-building firm and many other industrial endeavours. To honour the memory of

25

with a story attached. The Shanghai Exhibition Hall, for example, was built in Russian style in 1954, with enormous, massive pillars and thick walls. But earlier, on that very site, stood a private residence with rooms arranged in courtyards in a garden in the traditional Chinese fashion. Known as the Daguanyuan (the fictional Jia family's Grand View Garden from the Qing-dynasty classic *A Dream of Red Mansions*) of the 1930s, it was owned by a wealthy Jewish merchant, Silars Aaron Hardoon, who started off working for the Sassoon family. His garden was the gathering point for a group of Chinese scholars and officials, a sort of cultural salon, which was given the name Cang Sheng, the "Sage University of Enlightenment".

Other houses, although not themselves anything out of the ordinary, are of interest because of the fame or notoriety of their former occupants. Among these are the house where Dr. Sun Yat-sen (1866-1925) lived briefly on Xiangshan Road, the residence of the writer Lu Xun (1881-1936) in the Hongkou District, the official residence of the Kuomintang general Park Chung Hee in Xuhui District, and the Dingxiang (Lilac) Garden on Huashan Road where the Qing minister Li Hongzhang, an Anhui warlord, kept his mistress.

Perhaps Park Chung Hee's residence is the most distinctive in style. The general was a devout Muslim and his official residence exhibits some of the special grace notes of Islamic architecture. The carved patterns and shapes of the window colonnades are especially reminiscent of the Middle East.

Strolling in the area where the districts of Jing'an, Luwan and Xuhui intersect, you come across many houses reminiscent of a Central European style surrounded by gardens, especially on Wuxing Road and Hengshan Road in Xuhui District. Not large, but comfortable, these houses have roofs laid with ochre-coloured tiles and often shutters on the windows. You also find individual houses and villas such as you might see in the French, Italian and English countryside, as well as large buildings topped with turrets and crenellations which look like a wicked queen's castle out of Grimms' Fairytales.

When we reached Fenyang Road in Xuhui District, we sighted a spacious mansion in a large garden. Built in a classical French style, the structure had a pillar-shaped facade which gave the entire building an imposing and solemn look. Two wide, symmetrically placed staircases rose along the curved outer wall. The interior of this mansion is most charming, with elegant stucco work around the doors, windows and ceilings. The creamy colour scheme in the rooms added to the sense of lightness and delicacy. We learned that this very European mansion, once the residence of a former mayor of Shanghai, Chen Yi, is now the site of the Shanghai Arts and Crafts Research Institute.

Eventually, we directed our steps to Xujiahui in the southwestern quarter of the city. The St. Ignatius Cathedral there, a neo-Gothic edifice built in 1906, is said to be the largest Catholic cathedral in the Far East. It suffered severe damage during the "cultural revolution" and has only been reopened to worshippers since November 1979. One of the special features of its architectural style, based on the sublime Gothic architecture of the 12th to 16th centuries in Europe, is its vertical emphasis. Accordingly, the cathedral has high, tapering steeples, lancet arches and ribbed vaults to show. The steeples are set to the right and left of the facade in absolute symmetry and are set off by four tiny turrets at each corner of their base.

But you cannot really appreciate the full atmosphere of the cathedral unless you enter and stand in the nave. Looking up, I noted how the individual segments of the vaulted roof interconnect, creating an inherently balanced, rhythmic pattern. An astray sunbeam poking through a yellow stained-glass window above the chancel flooded the entire nave with light. All the proportions of the interior space in the cathedral are such as to emphasize this vertical thrust, as though the architect was focusing all one's attention on the heavens above, on the "Kingdom of God".

Translated by Ren Jiazhen

1. The neo-Gothic St. Ignatius Catholic Cathedral (by Wang Gangfeng).
2. European villas in Jing'an District offer ideal picturesque studies for talented young painters.
3. The Islamic touch is evident in the design of Park Chong Hee's residence in Xuhui District.

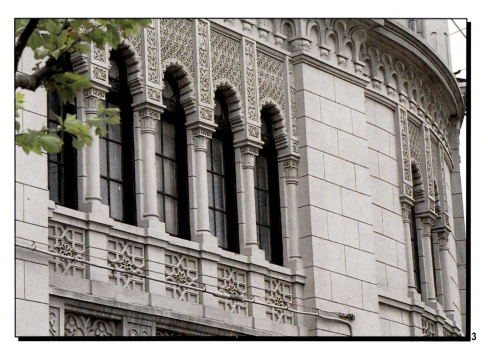

Shanghai's Kaleidoscopic Changes

PHOTOS BY XIE GUANGHUI
ARTICLE BY YU FENG

During the rush hour Shanghai is inevitably inundated in an ocean of bicycles no matter what is being done to ease the traffic jams.

Talk of Shanghai's development, and the familiar line leaps to mind: "A new look every year; a major change every three years." On my way to visit the city after a departure of exactly three years, this line kept me wondering what had really become of Shanghai during my absence.

The first thing that came in sight when the plane touched down at Hongqiao Airport was the terminal building. More palatial and imposing than I remembered, it had changed beyond recognition. My friend who came to meet me said that the building had just been expanded to cover twice as large a floor space. I had hardly finished marvelling at this quick speed of construction he chipped in, "You'll see more such things which seem to have appeared overnight." He reeled off one name after another: Yangpu and Nanpu, the world's first and second largest cable-braced bridges; the "Pearl of the Orient", Asian's tallest TV tower; the Bund, which had just been widened by several dozen metres into the Huangpu River; the newly refurbished People's Square and Xujiahui Plaza; the Manketon Tower; and many more.

His introduction made me itch to see it all. However, on my way to the hotel, my attention was attracted by the fashionable clothes people were wearing in the streets.

Fashion: Up to World Standards

Shanghai has all along been the leader in Chinese fashion. As the saying goes, "When eating, go to Guangzhou; when buying clothing, Shanghai is the place." As a native of Hong Kong, I had the impression that a few years ago Shanghai was still trailing behind the world's latest fashion. This time around, I saw little different between Shanghai and Hong Kong in this regard. What the ladies were wearing were as classy and elegant as anywhere in the world, whether in style, material or ornamentation. Women of Shanghai are mostly fair of skin, graceful of looks and well-cultured in etiquette. In attire they are conscious of personality, taste and quality. Though looking quite similar to what I had seen in Paris, Tokyo or Hong Kong a short while before, the fashion of Shanghai was imbued with a subtly Oriental elegance. The world's newest fads, too, have found their way into this burgeoning cosmopolitan city, thanks, among other things, to those world famous transnational companies which have set up shops there, bringing in such brand names as Pierre Cardin, Lacoste/Crocodile, Michel Rene and Esprit.

More than half a century ago, foreigners came in flocks to Shanghai, then a de facto colony known as a

1. *A moment of romance, witnessed by a camera crew filming for a commercial advertising atop Shanghai's Jinmen Hotel (by Er Dongqiang).*

2. *With an expensive pet in tow, a fashionable lady takes a walk along the Bund.*

3. *Luxury cars are a dime a dozen in Shanghai nowadays, an indication that the current economic boom has spawned a new generation of rich people.*

4. *The reappearance of rickshaws after decades of absence adds a nostalgic touch to Shanghai's landscape.*

Pictures of Hong Kong singing stars who are adored by the younger generation in Shanghai are posted in this dressing room of a group of young actresses.

A traditional department store is also decorated with the Western classical style statue in its entrance in order to attract more customers.

the begone days. Not to be outdone, Zhang Yimou, another famous Chinese film director, recently produced a film about old Shanghai under the title *Farewell, Shanghai.*

This nostalgia complex has also found expression in the emergence of an old men's jazz band. In the dim light of the tavern of the Peace Hotel (formerly Cathay) Hotel, the light shone colourful beams on the wrinkled faces of members of this band. A warm feeling, reminiscent of a time long past, was palpable in the melodious music they were playing. The players used to work in Shanghai's various dancing halls and cabarets in the 1940s. Four decades later today, when they reunited in the Peace Hotel to form this new jazz band, they proved they were still the best jazz players anywhere in the country. Faithfulness to the authentic flavour of this outlandish genre of music is a precious hallmark of this band, and precisely for this reason it did not take long for the band to win the hearts of Shanghai's old-timers, many of whom had returned after living overseas for many years. No less successful is another old men's jazz band playing in the Bailemen Nightclub. Its audience consists almost entirely of business people from Taiwan — some of them, having rediscovered this haunt of their former days, make it a point to be there every night. Plush and gilt saloons, cabarets and taverns have

"paradise for adventurers" with its land carved up between Britain, France, Japan, Germany and other big powers. Today, the city is receiving another major influx of foreigners, but the circumstances have changed. They are bringing the funds needed to speed up the city's development. European and American influences are back as well, which evokes memories of the Shanghai of the 1930s. This phenomenon prompted Chen Kaige, a well-known Chinese film director, to change the setting of his new film, *Wind and Moon,* from Nanjing to Shanghai of

mushroomed all over Shanghai in the last few years. There are over 3,000 of them now.

Stock Market and Automatic Cash Machines

Some Disco Squares are mostly white-collar workers of Sino-foreign joint ventures, but there is no lack of wheeler-dealers from Shanghai's stock market. The erratic fluctuations on the stock market and the pressure of the workplace drive them there in search of relaxation and respite.

The stock market is a much talked-of topic among Shanghai residents nowadays. The city's stock exchange centre is always crowded. Even its front door is mobbed by share-holders. With their eyes riveted on the giant TV screen in the hall, they are ready to transmit home by mobile phone what market changes they can detect. This scene is recaptured in the recent popular film *Stock Craze,* which tells the vivid story of an ordinary Shanghai woman who wants to hit the jackpot by speculating on the stock market. Emerging hand in hand with the stock market is the resuscitation of the city's money-changing industry. Markets dealing in futures in cereals and edible oils, coal, petroleum and agricultural capital goods have taken shape. People are writing cheques instead of paying cash while shopping in major stores or dining in large restaurants. The savings deposits cheque book is nothing new to Shanghai, where it was in circulation decades ago. Having reappeared in the mid-1980s, it is acquiring an expanding number of holders and becoming another important means of payment besides cash, credit cards and industrial and commercial cheques. A campaign is under way to attract Golden Card users by expanding the scope of its use in stores. Automatic machines recently made their debut in Shanghai streets.

This man, instead of inheriting the trade of his father, a paint baron, he prefers to earn his own living by working as a painter. He has established a private art gallery called the Garden Art Gallery in his own residence.

Aspiring film stars — students of a private performing art school opened in Shanghai by Xie Jin, an preeminent Chinese movie director.

The programmes presented by the Old Jazz Band in Peace Hotel are welcomed with a feeling of nostalgia (by Chan Yat Nin).

1

2

1. Shanghai is one of China's two major stock exchange markets. (The other one is Shenzhen.) The ups and downs of the stock market tug at many hearts in this city (by Zhou Wenhua).

2. In order to boost the company's celebrity, Shanghai New World Health Beverage Co. Ltd. has hired the 2.37-metre-tall Zhang Juncai as a member of its Public Relation Department (by Liu Jiaxiang)

3. Cheng Pulin, a dramatist, has become one of the real etare dealers and pet-dog owners (by Chen Haiwen).

4. The local residents' high expectations of their children, coupled with the rapid increase in the number of children of foreign employees, have given rise to elite private schools. The Shanghai Yaozhong International School is one such institution, attended by students from China and abroad.

5. Shanghai has a vast pool of talent. Enjoying the freedom provided by reform, they are able to choose the jobs they like most. On this job market, prospective employers and employees hunt for each other.

6. An auto exhibition is held by dozens of foreign auto companies at Shanghai National Trade Centre, and a "brand-name car with famous model" photo contest is also held for adverstising (by Tang Zaiqing).

Nanjing Road — Shoppers' Mecca

Both Nanjing Road and Huaihai Road are Shanghai's well-known shopping streets. Also known as "No. 1 Commercial Street in China", Nanjing Road features a hundred or so old stores selling such brand-name products as Zhang Xiaoquan's scissors; Old Jiefu's woollen fabrics; Wang Xing's fans; Peiluomeng Western-style suits; Hengdeli clocks; Maochang glasses; Lantang leather shoes; and Hongxiang ladies' wear. Each of the brand names is steeped in the street's time-honoured tradition. The addition of Shanghai No. 1 Department Store and the Hualian Shopping Mall have turned the five-kilometre street into an all-inclusive commercial establishment which seems perpetually packed with shoppers. In 1993 alone its sales totalled two billion yuan.

Unlike Nanjing Road which seems to be occupied by visitors from all corners of the country, Huaihai Road remains the local people's own shopping street. The miscellaneous merchandise on sale there is guaranteed to be of fine craftsmanship and high quality. The road has just undergone a major facelift, during which a number of European-style restaurants and hotels were added to provide a more pleasant environment for consumers. Competition has intensified, as a dozen large transnational companies have earned a niche in the road. Fresh fruit from the United States, Australia, Thailand, Malaysia and Japan are on sale along with native Chinese products in the street's largest food store. The World Shoe and Hat Store is selling British gentlemen's hats, French berets and an assortment of ladies' hats from various countries. East and West also meet in the beauty parlors, gift shops, garment stories and restaurants that line the road. A stroll along Huaihai Road brings memory of the tree-lined Champs-Elysees of Pairs, the colourful Marunouchi District of Tokyo and Manhattan in New York.

Eating and Shopping at the City God's Temple

It was when I became famished and started looking for a restaurant after a hectic day of window-shopping

3

4

that I realized Shanghai was also a gastronomes' paradise. The Chinese restaurants there belong to every school of Chinese cuisine — Sichuan, Hunan, Cantonese, Jiangsu, and what not. Many Western-style restaurants have been established in the city as well; the Deda Restaurant and Swans Tower are two of them. There are a host of fast food chains, such as Kentucky Fried Chicken, Californian Beef Noodle, Shanghai Ronghua Chicken, Minor Shaoxing Chicken, Zhengding Chicken, Muzi Chicken, Taiwan's Mei You Mei and Hong Kong's Dong Dong. For snacks there are the Nanxiang stuffed buns, dumplings stuffed with shrimp meat and fermented snail meat. The Daqian Gourmet World in Xujiahui offers delicacies from all over the world. People in Shanghai are becoming more and more choosy about what they eat, and they take increasing notice of the rare and the exotic and for the cultural implications behind what they eat. The catch phrase now, however, is "return to nature", so wild vegetables have come into vogue. But one thing is unmistakable that their eating habits are becoming increasingly globalist.

As a personal choice I decided to stick to local delicacies. That was why I drove all the way to the City God's Temple, where I entered an old restaurant and treated myself to cooked sausage with lucerne, "eight-treasure" with spicy sauce, soybean soup with pork slices and a number of other exotic local dishes.

I was in for a big surprise when I visited my favourite place, the old shopping mall beside the City God's Temple. The cluster of old, dilapidated stores have disappeared and given way to an imposing structure known as the Yuyuan Shopping Mall.

Built in the style of a royal palace with upturned eaves, carved pillars and painted beams, the shopping mall sells the same stuff as before, ranging from pottery teapots and carved ivory chopsticks to a kind of candy made of pear paste. There the buyer can always find things they cannot elsewhere. In the vicinity a zigzag bridge conducts to a pavilion built in the centre of a small lake, where pink lotus flowers were in full blossom. Behind the walls of the Yuyuan Park opposite the temple someone was playing a traditional Chinese stringed musical instrument. In the gentle breeze the poignant and sweet notes of the music could be heard faintly, reminding me that Shanghai was part of the State of Yue during the Warring States Period more than 1,000 years ago.

Translated by Ling Yuan

3

4

5

1. A wedding photo studio owned by a Taiwanese is doing roaring business. Couples line up for their turn.

2. A booming manufacturing industry has turned Shanghai into a paradise for shoppers. While new shopping malls appear one after another, many old stores have new looks to woo customers. By incorporating foreign capital, the old Hongxiang Department Store is now selling world-famous garments for a several thousand yuan apiece (by Chan Yat Nin).

3. A large fast food outlet, situated on the ground floor of the Daqian Gourmet World in the newly transformed Xujiahui Square.

4. In a bid to lure diners, managers have fashioned the Guo Xiang Restaurant into the shape of an ocean-going ship.

5. As born entrepreneurs Shanghai residents have invented a thousand and one ways of selling their wares. Here a cartoon is erected to attract the attention of prospective buyers.

The New Bund — Where Gold Flows and Colours Sparkle

ARTICLE BY SHENG ZHI

A steady stream of people come to do setting-up exercises on the embankment of the Bund in the early morning (by Xie Guanghui).

Facing page: *The enlarged and rebuilt Bund is cleaner and as beautiful as a riverfront park next to the 10-lane motorway. The signal station at the end of East Yan'an Road has been ingeniously preserved during reconstruction. It now stands between the widened road and the embankment (by Chan Yat Nin).*

From top to bottom:

• *Traffic along the Bund is even heavy at night (by Xie Guanghui).*

• *The Bund in the 1940s. Company and bank buildings stood in a continuous line and the riverfront was lined with docks and land transportation stations (CT archives).*

• *The signal station facing the entrance to present-day East Yan'an Road on the Bund was built in 1902 to hoist weather signs and guide ships on the Huangpu River. It has been preserved as a historical relic (CT archives).*

The Bund is the most famous sightseeing spot in Shanghai. The Waibaidu Bridge, the long embankment along the Huangpu River and the imposing array of tall buildings known as "an international architectural exhibition" together form a symbol of the great metropolis of the East. The Bund has always been closely linked with the development of Shanghai. In the last three years, the Bund has undergone great changes that surprise even the native Shanghainese — it has suddenly become wider, bigger and more beautiful.

The "Lovers' Wall" Is Replaced by a New Embankment

A chest-high wall used to stand along the embankment of the Huangpu River. This was the famous "Lovers' Wall", known throughout the country. On summer evenings, innumerable pairs of lovers would stand along the wall whispering words of love to each other. As there were so many couples, there could hardly tell which two were a pair.

Three years ago, this long-standing flood-prevention cement wall was pulled down. The shabby narrow brick-paved embankment is also no more. It has been replaced by a wider and higher new embankment. The highest tier of the new two-tier embankment is paved with polished marble, protected by a beautiful metal guardrail and illuminated by classically styled gas lights spaced at regular intervals. Leaning on the guardrail, as the river flows below, one can enjoy a panoramic view of the ships and boats plying the river and the high-rise buildings of Pudong on the opposite bank. On the street-side of the embankment are wide beds of greenery and marble benches. People can now take a leisurely stroll on the embankment, lean on the guardrail or sit on the benches to enjoy a broader sight instead of being squeezed against one another along the old wall. Flights of steps lead down to another tier of the embankment several hundred metres in length, where one can stroll or sit in the shade of green trees and watch the morass of vehicles along the waterfront street. Underground pedestrian crossings lead to the other side of the street.

New Scenes Along the New Bund

The street near the Waibaidu Bridge has also been much widened. The Huangpu Park near the bridge has become part of the embankment and a city park open to everybody. A terrace has been built on the riverfront side of the park, on which stands a martyr's monument surrounded by evergreen pines and firs. Over half a century ago, there was, at the gate of this very park, a sign that said, "No admittance to Chinese and dogs."

This newly sculpted statue at the Bund is in perfect harmony with the buildings erected early this century (by Liu Bingyuan).

Two bronze lions, exactly the same as the pair at the Hong Kong and Shanghai Banking Corporation in Hong Kong, used to stand in front of the former Hong Kong and Shanghai Banking Corporation building in Shanghai. They were moved to a museum long ago (CT archives).

The Shanghai Municipal Government is housed in the former Hong Kong and Shanghai Banking Corporation building. Once extolled as "the most magnificent structure in the East", the building still retains some of its former glory today. It will soon change owners and be converted back into a financial and bank building (by Chan Yat Nin).

The former Hong Kong and Shanghai Banking Corporation building at the entrance to Fuzhou Road on the Bund was first built in 1880 and reconstructed at the original site into what it is like today in 1923. This imposing edifice stands on a solid granite foundation. Its portico and tall baroque columns are neoclassical in style (CT archives).

Every morning, employees from the offices along the Bund come out to sweep the street in front of their offices. This way of keeping public places clean is typical of the present day (by Xie Guanghui).

The new Bund is several times bigger in space and size than the Bund of yesteryear. To clear the Bund, a number of structures, including the municipal hydrographic station have been pulled down and moved away.

The more spacious Bund is now frequented from morning till night. In the early morning, before the mists on the river are dispelled, older people come in groups to the embankment to practise Taiji Boxing and sword exercises, or perform a rhythmic disco-dance while enjoying the fresh morning air by the green trees and river waters. As soon as these older people leave at eight or nine, their places are filled by visitors to the city. From their clothing, skin colour and accent, one can tell they are not Shanghainese but people from other parts of the country. They usually carry bundles with them, which betray the fact they have just completed a shopping tour at nearby Nanjing Road, No. 1 Commercial Street in China. Mixed among these visitors are also golden-haired and blue-eyed foreign tourists. Most of the people who come to the Bund in the evening are young lovers. During weekends, there is often an open-air orchestral performance given by Shanghai's instrumental musicians in front of the bronze statue of Chen Yi, the first mayor of the Shanghai Municipal People's Government. Their performance adds an air of elegance to the bustling city in the evening.

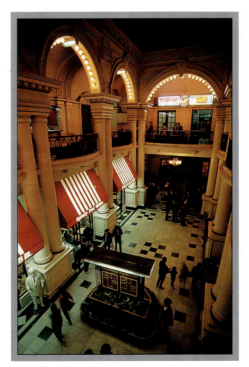

Gold rush: Kentucky occupies a prime location on the ground floor of the illustrious Dong Feng Building, Shanghai (by Chan Yat Nin).

Buildings Along the New Bund

The kaleidoscopic night scene of the new Bund is the pride of the Shanghainese. The tall buildings standing along one side of the riverfront street are outlined by colourful electric lights. Reflecting off the green lawns and trees below, these lights make the differently styled buildings look like magnificent castles in fairy tales — a sight that cannot be found anywhere else in China. The most prominent among the buildings are the Bank Building and Peace Hotel. Built by the British-Jewish businessman Sassoon, the Peace Hotel has a history of nearly a hundred years and was originally named the Sassoon Building. When the Bank Building was erected later by the old Bank of China, Sassoon forcibly prevented it from exceeding the height of the spire of the Sassoon Building so that his building would remain the tallest in the city. Today, illuminated by pale purple lights, the two stone buildings stand as testimonies to the tumultuous history of the Bund over the last hundred years.

Standing on the Bund, one has a clear view

Spotlights along the Bund were installed in the 1990s (by Xie Guanghui).

A Huangpu Tourist Festival is held every year. The section of the Bund at East Nanjing Road is the centre of festivities. Do the revellers know that the Peace Hotel in the background was the famous Sassoon Building in the old days? (by Xie Guanghui).

The Sassoon building with its neat and clean outlines and pyramidal roof is structured in the early modern style. Built in 1928 by Sassoon, at the turn of the century, it has become a historical landmark in Shanghai (CT archives).

The memorial statue of Sir Harry Smith Parkes (1828-1885), British minister to China, erected in 1890, was demolished by the Japanese army when Shanghai was occupied during World War II. Also destoyed were the statue of Sir Robert Hart (1835-1911) in front of the Customs Building and the Peace Monument at East Yan'an Road built in memory of those foreign residents in Shanghai who fought and were killed in World War I (CT archives).

The statue of Chen Yi (1901-1972), the first mayor of Shanghai of the People's Republic of China, now overlooks a crowd of dancers on the Bund at the end of Nanjing East Road every morning (by Chan Yat Nin).

of the Dongfang Mingzhu (The Pearl of the Orient) TV Tower piercing into the blue sky on the far opposite bank of the Huangpu River. The TV tower, 468 metres high, is the third tallest in the world, next to the TV tower of Toronto and Moscow's Ostendin TV tower, and is the tallest in Asia. At night, the TV tower is transformed into a colourful column of lights with two large multicoloured spheres on top, supported by three huge pillars. Between the two spheres is a six-sectioned board of lights, which changes between into silvery white, jade green or dreamy purple. Programmed by computer, the sequence in which the lights change colour is different every day. Completed on the eve of the National Day on October 1, 1994, the TV tower has become a new attraction on the Bund.

From "Golden Sector" to Financial Street

The Bund was already the "golden sector" of the city over half a century ago, when more than a hundred bank buildings congregated here. Today, as Shanghai's historically powerful financial establishments are reasserting themselves, they have once again chosen the Bund. Through exchange, public bidding and auctioning, the buildings along the Bund will gradually be allocated to Chinese and foreign financial establishments. At the moment, a considerable number of Chinese financial companies and more than 20 foreign ones are frantically making a dash for a place there. The China Foreign Currency Exchange at Building No. 15 of the Bund went into operation on April 4, 1994. Within 10 days, nearly one billion US dollars worth of foreign currencies changed hands there. This shows that Shanghai's foreign currency market is still the "dragon head" of the country, though the headquarters of most of the big banks are concentrated in Beijing. Following the birth of Shanghai's Financial Exchange on the Bund, future trading in grain, oil, coal, agricultural capital goods and petroleum is also gradually forming its own market. As the Bund transforms itself into China's "Wall Street", gold will flow and colour will really sparkle there.

Translated by Tang Bowen

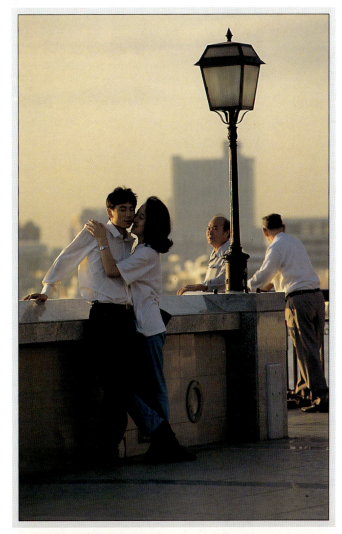
Lovers line up along the so-called Lovers' Wall along the Bund at all times of the day (by Xie Guanghui).

A Natural Barrier Has Turned into a Thoroughfare?

PHOTOS BY XIE GUANGHUI
ARTICLE BY ZHU RUI

Vessels busily shuttle on the Huangpu River under the Yangpu Bridge — the largest cable-braced bridge in the world.

The Nangpu bridge approach is in beautiful spirals.

The Huangpu River was a natural barrier between the Shanghai people, which divided Shanghai into two parts — the East and the West, forming a strange phenomenon: While the western part had become very prosperous, the eastern part still remained undeveloped. In people's mind, Puxi (the western part) represented the prosperous Shanghai, and Pudong — the other half of Shanghai — seemed to have been forgotten by people consciously or unconsciously. In history, many prominent personages had made proposals to develop Pudong, but none of their proposals were realized because of the natural barrier of the Huangpu River. When Puxi had become a most resplendent pearl in the Far East several decades ago, Pudong was still a deserted beach, where only the tidal water of the river came to wash away the loneliness.

With the passage of time, Puxi became increasingly small to cope with Shanghai's development and the expansion of its economy and urban construction. Shanghai became a very crowded city, with each inch of its soil worth 10 inches of gold. But Pudong, just on the other side of the river, remained a vast expanse of virgin land waiting to be developed. In the old times people going from Pudong to Puxi or from Puxi to Pudong relied on sampans to ferry the river. Later they changed to ferry steamers. In the early 1980s, the Dapuqiao Tunnel, which had been dug for military use, was opened to public traffic. But to a city like Shanghai where the economy developed by leaps and bounds, this measure was so inadequate that it was just like trying to put out a burning cartload of faggots with a cup of water. So Shanghai people felt hopeless and frustrated when they gazed at the vast expanse of land just on the opposite bank of the river. The Huangpu River had flowed through Shanghai as a city for 700 years, and the Shanghai people had dreamed of having a bridge over it for 700 long years.

Today, Shanghai people's dream has come true as two large bridges — the Nanpu Bridge and the Yangpu Bridge — have been built on the Huangpu River.

The Nanpu Bridge, located at Shanghai's Southern Docks, was the first bridge built on the Huangpu River. As the world's third largest double-tower cable-braced bridge, it has a total length of 8,346 metres, with its cross section being 846 metres and its main span 423 metres. Its main towers are in an "H" shape, each 150 metres high. On either side of the towers are 22 pairs of steel cables connecting the main beams. The chains are arranged in the shape of a fan. The main bridge flooring is 30.35 metres wide, with six traffic lanes in the middle and a two-metre wide sidewalk on either side for pedestrians and sightseers. The bridge approach is 7,500 metres long. The section of the bridge approach in Puxi is 3,754 metres long and in spirals. It branches off in the upper and lower rings and connects South Zhongshan Road and Lujiabin Road respectively. The section of the bridge approach in Pudong is 3,746 metres long, which runs straight eastward to link up with Yangyao Highway and connect the two ends of South Pudong Road through two elliptical circles. At either end of the bridge there is an elevator tower over 50 metres high for sightseers.

From top to bottom:

• *The section of the Yanpu bridge approach with rotary intersection (by Chan Yat Nin)*

• *The bridge towers and the cables look like a huge harp.*

• *The bridges have become new attractions for sightseers and lovers.*

Eleven kilometres from the Nanpu Bridge there is the Yangpu Bridge, which is 7,658 metres long, with its main span being 602 metres. It is the world's largest suspension bridge. Since completion, the two bridges have become two tourist attractions in Shanghai and, with their beautiful shapes, unique styles and imposing features, have drawn people to come to visit in endless streams.

If you climb up the TV Tower of the "Pearl of the Orient" and look to the distance in a clear autumn afternoon, a magnificent scene will come into view: the dragon-like Yangpu and Nanpu great bridges loom high up in the air spanning the Huangpu River; the huge bridge towers and the slanting cables like a splendid stave in the horizon, and boats shuttling to and fro on the narrowed river look like the notes on the stave. At dusk, if you walk on the bridges, you will find yourself bathed together with the bridges in the afterglow of the setting sun and tinged with a light red layer of brilliance, and you will feel that you have become a part of the scenery. If you lean over the rails and look down, you will see the river surge forward with golden waves in the setting sun. Sirens sound, and hundreds of vessels, including 50,000-ton ships, pass by. Viewed from a distance at night, the two bridges under the illumination of myriad of lamps look like two huge, ever-rising rings of light inlaid on the dark velvet curtain of the sky.

Today, the natural barrier has turned into a thoroughfare. Besides the bridges, tunnels that run across the river were also dug at East Yan'an Road and other places a few years ago. Now, a new project has begun to extend the tunnels, and the third magnificent suspension bridge on the Huangpu River — the Xupu Bridge — is under construction and will be completed and open to traffic in 1996.

Now, Pudong and Puxi, the two parts of Shanghai, have integrated into a graphic whole and will become prosperous together.

Translated by Xiong Zhenru

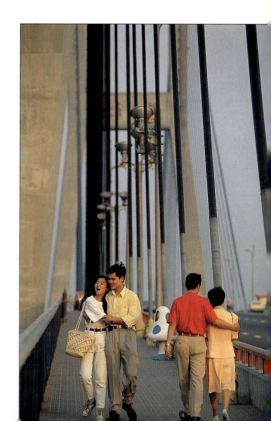

A Glimpse of Pudong

ARTICLE BY ZHU RUI

The narrow Huangpu River divides Shanghai into two parts — Pudong and Puxi. Though only a river apart, Pudong and Puxi were two entirely different worlds in the past. On the bund of Puxi stands groups of buildings of multi-national styles representing the pride of Shanghai, while Pudong was a desolate land or as Shanghainese put it, "a rural area". Hence, local nicknames of places such as "muddy ferry", "garbage pile", and "foundry shop" are reminders of Pudong's past. A popular saying went, "A bed in Puxi is better than a room in Pudong", is an accurate image of the old Pudong in Shanghai minds.

A Springboard into the 21st Century

Today Pudong has become the hot topic in Shanghai. News about Pudong pours in every day. Instead of Nanjing Road, the City of God Temple and the Bund, people now take visitors to Pudong for sightseeing. Pudong has become the pride of Shanghai.

Soon after the announcement of the decision to develop and open up Pudong, the accompanying 10 favourable policies and five exclusive policies in 1990, Pudong was immediately pushed to the forefront of China's economic reforms. From then on, Pudong has attracted people's attention. Yet Pudong's opening up has not been so sensational as the early development days of Shenzhen's Special Economic Zone, nor so spectacular as when 100,000 people crossed the Qiongzhou Straits to Hainan Island. Pudong, however, has quietly risen like a star east of Shanghai. In a short space of four years, 10 large infrastructure projects costing 20 billion yuan have been basically completed; construction of financial, bonded and two other development areas are in full swing. Commercial buildings along the Zhangyang Road, equal to two Nanjing roads, are under construction. Huge investments from other parts of the country and abroad are pouring into Pudong, and well-known multi-national corporations come to invest .... As a matter of fact, today's Pudong has become a new springboard for Shanghai into the 21st century.

The Pearl of the Orient TV Tower

When visiting Shanghai you will inevitably be introduced to the 468-metre high TV tower which ranks first in Asia and third in the world for its sheer height. Familiarly known as the Pearl of the Orient, it is a landmark to Shanghainese just as the Sydney Opera House is to Australians and the Eiffel Tower to the French. The designer's inspiration, however, was derived from a line written by Bai Juyi, a prominent Tang-dynasty poet. The line goes, "It was like large and small pearls dropping on a plate of jade." Looking up from the base of the tower, you can distinctly see 11 large and small sized pearl-like shining balls, decorating the tower. The upper and lower balls and the spaceship are the big simulated pearls. It takes only 40 seconds by elevator to reach the upper ball which is 263 metres above ground and has a diameter of 45 metres. It is actually a sightseeing hall. Through the glass panes of the revolving dining-hall you can have a panoramic view of Shanghai. Down below, the Huangpu River flows past the tower like a jade ribbon, Pudong Park looks like an exquisite jade plate and the Nanpu and Yangpu Bridge arch over the Huangpu River like a rainbow. If it is a fine day you can even see Chongming Island and the Yangtse estuary in the distance. The lower ball with a diameter of 50 metres will become a large amusement centre for children. Between the two big balls are five small balls. They and the three other small balls hung on three supporting pillars are actually hotels in the air, where each small ball has five suites. At night, lit up by laser flood and lights, the Pearl of the Orient TV Tower is resplendent and dazzling to the eye.

Lujiazui — The New Bund of Pudong

The Pearl of the Orient TV Tower is located in the Lujiazui Financial Area.

3

Though lying opposite to the old financial area on the bund of Puxi, it has slumbered for at least 350 years since it was named Lujiazui in 1544, during the Qing Dynasty. Almost in one night it has gained a new eminence.

On the map, Pudong with an area of 518 square kilometres is shaped just like the profile of a beautiful girl, and Lujiazui her straight nose. The Huangpu River carves out an arc or a bend here. It is a masterpiece of Mother Nature. Lujiazui is now the only development area in China that is named "the financial and trade area". It will focus on developing tertiary industry including finance, trade, commerce and information and consultation. It will be the hub linking Pudong and Puxi, and the nucleus of the up-and-coming Pudong area. By 2010, Lujiazui will become a financial centre and the symbol of new Shanghai. In just three years of development, the area has attracted billions of US dollars in investment, building up a com-

1. The design of "The Pearl of the Orient" TV Tower embodies the poem from Bai Juyi: "It was like large and small pearls dropping on a plate of jade" (by Xie Guanghui).
2. Luoshan Bridge is the revolving hub of the newly-built inner ring route expressway, which links Nanpu Bridge to Yangpu Bridge (by Liu Kaiming).
3. Break with the past: the laying of foundation stones is a ceremony commonly witnessed in today's Pudong with its many new projects (by Lu Heping).

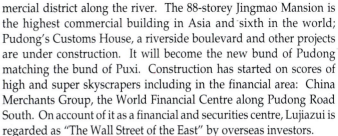

mercial district along the river. The 88-storey Jingmao Mansion is the highest commercial building in Asia and sixth in the world; Pudong's Customs House, a riverside boulevard and other projects are under construction. It will become the new bund of Pudong matching the bund of Puxi. Construction has started on scores of high and super skyscrapers including in the financial area: China Merchants Group, the World Financial Centre along Pudong Road South. On account of it as a financial and securities centre, Lujiazui is regarded as "The Wall Street of the East" by overseas investors.

A Sino-Japanese venture, Shanghai's first Yaohan, Asia's biggest supermarket, is located on the commercial high street of Zhangyang Road. In addition, there is the internal trade area Zhuyuan, and five functional districts of Longyang comprehensive commodity area. All these are scattered along the planned axis of Pudong. After visiting Lujiazui, an overseas banker forecasted that it would be the international capital market of the 21st century.

The Simultaneous Development of Commercial and Tourist Areas

The Waigaoqiao Bonded Area, the first of its kind in China, offers free trade and processing for exports came into operation in 1993. The 10-square-kilometre bonded area is now enclosed by silvery steel wires. To enter it you have to go through procedures at Customs House. For the time being the processing district is the most prosperous in Waigaoqiao. Over 90% of the land has been rented out or transferred and hundreds of overseas investment projects have been started. Moreover, many of the overseas investors such as JVC have successfully expanded in their operations and presence in the district. What is particularly noteworthy is the Shanghai Park View, a Shanghai-Hong Kong joint venture which is based on Hong Kong's famous Park View. Upon completion it will comprise of a five-star hotel and over a dozen commercial and residential buildings providing a place for offices, recreation and residents.

1. Lujiazui will become an international financial market in the 21st century (by Xie Guanghui).
2. Residences in Pudong have sprung up like mushrooms (by Xie Guanghui).
3. The town of Gaoqiao will soon have a new facelift (by Xie Guanghui).
4. The old pace of life in Pudong, but how long will it last? (by Lu Yuanmin)
5. When completed, Waigaoqiao Bonded Area will become the first of its kind in China's system of free trade (by Xie Guanghui).
6. A dense port in Huangpu River, Pudong (by Lu Yun).
7. Pudong's trading and shipping has brought many foreigners to the area. This restaurant is a favourite haunt of Cuban crew and businessmen as testified by signatures on the wall (by Lu Heping).

Today, old hands of the international commercial circle are gathering at the Jinqiao Export Processing District. On average, each square metre has attracted an investment of over US$900, topping the list of China's development zones. Colourful banners and buildings in exotic styles can be seen everywhere such as Mitsubishi, Siemens, Bayer... Investors from Hong Kong, Australia and Taiwan are particularly interested and have invested in over 50 of the 200 plus projects under construction.

Just as people are focussing their attention on financial trade and high-tech areas, the Huaxia Commercial and Tourist Area is being mapped out. In the not too distant future there will emerge in the coastal Shanjia harbour area, a high-standard Huaxia Beach Tourist Area with a water paradise covering an area of 150 hectares, and seaside villas totalling over 100 hectares. There will also be an immense Huaxia Commercial district occupying 62 hectares and a huge Miniature Entertainment Centre taking prominent historical personages and legendary stories as its themes.

A bridge for Shanghai and the rest of China to march into the 21st century, the developing Pudong will once again fill the Shanghainese with pride: leading the world trends.

Translated by Anne Yan

Smiling faces are seen everywhere on the streets at night.

Night in Shanghai

PHOTOS BY XIE GUANGHUI
TEXT BY ZHU RUI

As night unfolds, busy and noisy Shanghai begins to slowly quieten down, and the streets and lanes which have been crammed by streams of people and trucks during the day now find an opportunity to take a breath and relax. Metropolitan Shanghai is adorning itself, and in a short period of time it will be appear with a new look: neon lights, floodlights, laser illuminators, and the various colourful lamps that are known as "Full Sky Stars" flash on with their glimmering, revolving beams of light. In contrast from the day, Shanghai now reveals itself as a world of its own — leisurely, graceful and serene.

Places such as the Bund and Nanjing Road — Shanghai Centre, and The Pearl of the Orient TV Tower on the other bank of the Huangpu River, are each fascinating in their own right. Even the several kilometre-long road which connects Nanjing Road and leads to Hongqiao International Airport, is dazzlingly illuminated. Along the long road stands several dozen modern buildings of different styles and outlines such as Shanghai Mansion, Shanghai International Equatorial Hotel, New Century Square, Rainbow Hotel and International Trade Centre, which glitter translucently under the illumination of floodlights, giving visitors a dream-like feeling whether one is just viewing from afar, or actually walking around inside.

The recreational centre on the eighth floor of the Portman Shangri-La Hotel in the Shanghai Mansion, has high international standards. The Shanghai Bund Nightclub at the Xietai Centre and the Dream Shanghai Night Club at the International Trade Centre, the Casablanca Dance Hall of the Cesar's Palace on 13th floor of the Rainbow Hotel; the Nightclub and the VIP Club — all these places remind people of the old Shanghai: the "Nightless City of the Orient", despite the fact that several decades have gone by and the appearance of the buildings have already been modernized. Have we entered an age of nostalgia? This question hovers when you enter the VIP Club. The instant you step through the door, you feel you have entered another period — two husky men, who look like valiant cavalrymen, stand on either side of the doorway. They wear riding boots on their feet, sashes over their shoulders, and tasselled helmets on their heads. The Karaoke-TV rooms are illuminated by yellow lights, and the window glass has a distinct cross design on it perhaps suggesting a secret symbol. In the lobby the tulips are in full bloom. This kind of esoteric and exotic scene-setting is typical of an evening from old Shanghai.

Garden is a recreational ground where illusions are created using modern technology. In the dim, quiet space, candles flicker, and the music fountain, or "water dance" in the words of the local manager, dances slowly and sweetly, casting a soporific spell. However, as

1. In new commercial centres not only there are various kinds of Chinese and foreign commodities on sale, but also live piano music. Commerce and music complement each other (by Chan Yat Nin).
2. Night is the golden time for lovers. These lovers in pairs are the envy of others.
3. Yunnan Road is known for its food, specializing in refreshments at night, and is popular by both ordinary citizens and the rich.
4. Waves of people roll on Nanjing Road — No. 1 Commercial Street in China.

1. The Temujin Barbecue Shop at Xujiahui draws customers with its unique flavour and baking style. Reservations are recommended as it is hard to get a seat here.
2. No visitors to Shanghai should miss the opportunity to go to the Bund and enjoy Shanghai's magnificence when the evening lights come on, hence the brisk business of renting binoculars.
3. Every night at the Bund, places that cater food and recreation also manage to permeate a kind of romantic atmosphere, combining the new with nostalgic feelings.
4. In the newly established open-air restaurant at the Bund, people while eating and drinking can enjoy night scenes under the evening lights.

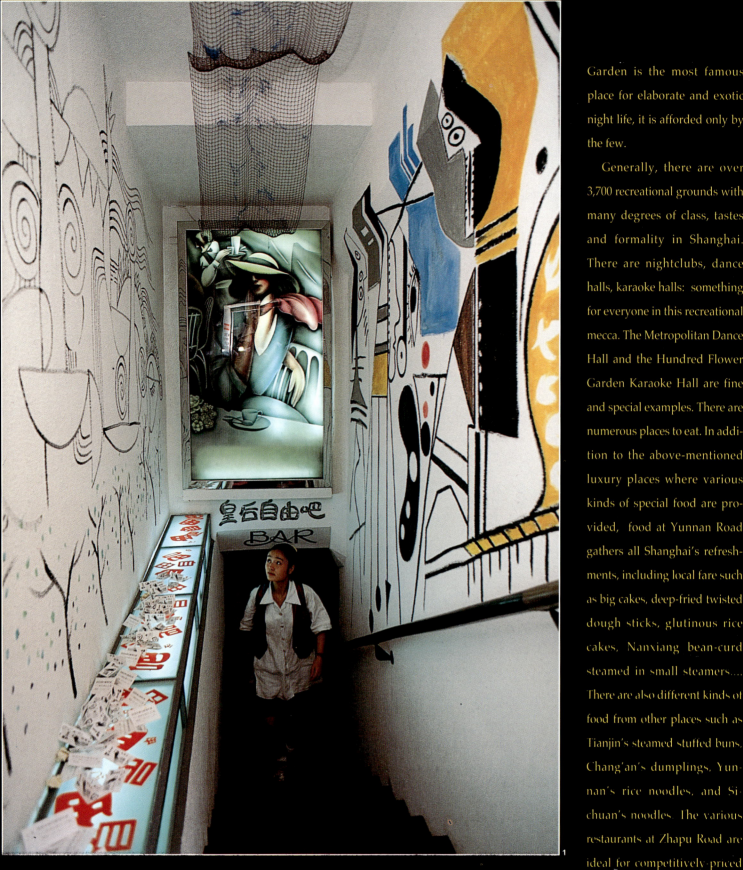

1. New bars are everywhere in Shanghai. This bar is located at the underground at Huaihai Road. Its uniquely decorated facade creates a surrealistic atmosphere.
2. Singing and dancing are more and more favourite in Shanghai. A stage is temporarily built on Xu Jiahui Square and many programmes are held to celebrate "Sweet-Scented Osmanthus Festival (by Xie Guanghui).
3. Luxury cars are often parked at places for night life; an indication of the high standards and tastes inside clubs, as set by today's consumers in Shanghai.
4. Conservative attitudes are no longer as strait-laced; today's young people in Shanghai date freely in public without fear of parental criticism.
5. The night life programmes presented by the Old Jazz Band in Peace Hotel are always welcomed by foreign guests. Many foreigners come to see their old friends in the jazz orchestra when they return on visits to Shanghai.

Garden is the most famous place for elaborate and exotic night life, it is afforded only by the few.

Generally, there are over 3,700 recreational grounds with many degrees of class, tastes and formality in Shanghai. There are nightclubs, dance halls, karaoke halls: something for everyone in this recreational mecca. The Metropolitan Dance Hall and the Hundred Flower Garden Karaoke Hall are fine and special examples. There are numerous places to eat. In addition to the above-mentioned luxury places where various kinds of special food are provided, food at Yunnan Road gathers all Shanghai's refreshments, including local fare such as big cakes, deep-fried twisted dough sticks, glutinous rice cakes, Nanxiang bean-curd steamed in small steamers.... There are also different kinds of food from other places such as Tianjin's steamed stuffed buns, Chang'an's dumplings, Yunnan's rice noodles, and Sichuan's noodles. The various restaurants at Zhapu Road are ideal for competitively-priced decent evening menus.

With the rise of evening breeze, Shanghai begins its multicoloured and fascinating night life.

Translated by Xiong Zhenru

A Paradise for Collectors

PHOTOS BY CHAN YAT NIN
ARTICLE BY DU KEDAO

1. The Fuyou Flea Market attracts crowds of amateur collectors every Sunday morning.
2. On the lookout for a wide variety of objects such as paintings and calligraphy
3. Pottery plant pots and shaped teapots
4. The better bargains may well be found in the street market, where haggling is the order of the day.
5. Auction sales are held at Shanghai's two newly reopened auction houses (by Er Dongqiang).
6. A small bronze ox with a round opening in its body

1. A typical store along Dongtai Road which specialises in antiques (by Xie Guanghui).
2. A store selling old clocks and watches

3. Collector Tao Rongxing and his wife are the owners of "Liquor Family Museum" (by Tang Zaiqing).
4. Collector Chen Baocai in his "Butterfly Specimens Family Museum"
5. Mini-sculptures and knickknacks collector, Zhou Changxing
6. Theatre costume collector, Bao Wanrong shares her interest with friends from the Beijing Opera

7. These knickknacks are made by Zhou Changxing himself
8. The valuable old coins collection is a favourite in Shanghai

A little after six in the morning and the sun's rays are just breaking through the darkness: Shanghai, Sunday morning. The dark silhouettes of people on bicycles or tricycles can be seen making for Fuyou Road, large and small packages dangling from their carriers.

Fuyou Road is one of the city's three main flea markets (the other two being at Dongtai Road and Zhonghua Xin Road). The market is held only on Sundays, beginning very early, so that from dawn onwards, traders are busy looking for the best spot on the pavement to unload and display their wares: curios, old clocks, coins, secondhand vases and jars.

As the sun rises, more people arrive, some pushing their loads on handcarts, and soon there are 800 or more pitches selling everything from ceramics, bronze and silverware, fans, medals and musical instruments, jade and cosmetic boxes, to woodcarvings, sofas and padauk furniture....

Among them are several items of Western origin, including a peep-show box resembling a pair of binoculars, which show small pictures through a magnifying lens in a small aperture. The refraction of light through the lens makes the picture look stereoscopic. These boxes were brought into China early this century and many the pictures have proved to be invaluable historical documents, showing street scenes of Old Shanghai.

At another pitch I spot an old-fashioned manual cash register next to a four-legged chamber pot with a large open top. Elsewhere there are a myriad other objects which the layman would find it more difficult to put a name to, such as a large barrel-shaped porcelain stand used for holding the black gauze headgear worn by the mandarins of old, or a strange bronze ox with a round opening in its body.

This flea market is reputed to be at least 100 years old, but its character has changed considerably over the period. It used to sell mainly used furniture, broken hardware and other bric-a-brac for which the owners had no further use. As time went on however and people became more prosperous, these items no longer interested anyone and objects with some collector's value such as padauk furniture, old clocks and watches, cultural relics and curios gradually replaced them.

Fuyou Road has thus become a regular haunt of amateur collector of all tastes, who come here early every Sunday morning on the lookout for rare or original objects. Business is brisk as they haggle with dealers in a language peculiar to the trade. For instance, when they say yi kuai (one yuan), they mean 100 yuan and wu jiao (half a yuan) means fifty yuan.

Unlike other Chinese markets, where people are noisy and unrestrained, transactions here are conducted in a very calm, quiet atmosphere. All potential customers give their undivided attention to appraising the goods they wish to buy, determining whether the articles are genuine or false, how much they are worth, etc. In turn the traders would not dream of pitching their wares at the top of their lungs, nor do they — they simply leave you alone to make your own decision. They keep quiet, waiting to see whether they are dealing with an experienced buyer, and only when you have picked up the object of your choice do they mention a figure — and the bargaining is conducted in whispered undertones.

One collector explains that he and his fellow devotees come to Fuyou Road early every Sunday morning, because only at this hour can a collector's piece be snapped up for a fairly low price. Customers are few and the competition less. Later in the morning, however, the traders are bound to raise their prices several times as more people evince an interest in the same piece. After 10 o'clock, the serious collectors having dispersed, the atmosphere becomes less strained and the field is left to the ordinary crowds strolling about curious to see what is on display.

But even a casual loiterer will become as keen as a "professional" collector should something really special catch his eye. Suppressing his excitement, he feigns a total lack of interest, even criticizing the item in question, before naming a price. After some haggling, the new owner walks away with his prize, a triumphant smile on his face.

This flea market also attracts foreign visitors, especially the wives of diplomats or expatriates resident in Shanghai. Today, a particular lady has found a pink porcelain plate and is arguing with the trader over whether she should pay for it in Renminbi or foreign currency. Others can be seen loading their cars with blue-and-white porcelain, padauk furniture, lacquerware and even carved night-stools.

Shanghai has numerous collection buffs. There are several hundred thousand people collecting over 100 different varieties of items, ranging from the six most popular — matchboxes, stamps, newspapers, coins, cigarette and wine bottle labels — to Chinese and foreign old clocks and watches, paintings and calligraphy by famous artists, antique porcelain, models of sailing boats, teapots, ivory minisculpture, ink slabs, ancient bronzes and stone seals, abacuses, chopsticks, fountain pens with gold nibs, antique locks and keys, butterfly specimens and envelopes with the handwriting of celebrities on them. The list is endless....

In recent years some of the more serious collectors have even set up small private museums in their own homes to exhibit their collections. This enthusiasm for collecting rare objects is difficult to sum up in a few words. From 1842, when Shanghai became a trading port, exposed to many outside influences, the prosperity of its inhabitants steadily increased. The wealthy then vied with each other in buying Chinese and foreign curios, paintings and calligraphy as tangible evidence of their high social standing. This trend grew to such an extent that Shanghai became known as "the custodian of half the rivers and mountains in the country". Later, under the impact of one historical event after another, objects collected by Shanghai's aristocratic families began to find their way into other hands, some were destroyed and others disappeared. Moreover, with the gradual improvement in economic conditions on the Chinese mainland in recent years, some people are beginning to have surplus money to hand, so much so that collecting rare objects has become a pastime not simply of the old upper classes but of the common people as well.

Two former auctioneer companies, Donghai and Donghua, have even resumed business, offering additional opportunities for collectors in search of rare objects (at one time 44 auctioneers were in business in Shanghai). Generally speaking, items sold at the auction are more valuable than those found at street markets.

Translated by Ren Jiazhen

1. Chen Baoding and his passion for abacuses. Abacuses are used to make the door of his shop.
2. In the Dongtai market most traders have their own shops.
3. One would have to be a true connoisseur to find a rare object amongst all this bric-a-brac.
4. Er Dongqiang examining objects from minority tribes.

Visiting Ancient Songjiang County Town

PHOTOS & ARTICLE BY CHAN YAT NIN

This small building stands in the old city, looking rather odd. Yet it is an ordinary residential building for the people of Songjiang.

Screen wall at the entrance of Zuibaichi. Relief on brick reveals the layout of the garden.

As the Yangtse River has continued its eternal flow from the mountains to the sea it has brought sand and mud from the inland regions of China and deposited them at its delta on the coast. Slowly the delta has expanded eastwards. As it has grown, so the fertile countryside has supported an ever increasing population. Yet the history of the Yangtse River Delta is not long. Shanghai became a county only 700 years ago and rose to become a major port city 100 years ago. But when talking about the history of Shanghai, the dragon head of the delta, people always like to mention the satellite town of Songjiang, which is ancient enough to boast a history exceeding several thousand years.

From Shanghai to this ancient town of Songjiang, the trip takes only one hour. Heading east, we soon spotted the tops of ancient pagodas rising above the buildings as we arrived at the county town. Entering the town, we came to a rivulet winding between the houses. Spanning the rivulet was a high stone arched bridge, its image reflected in the water below. The sound of oars greeted us as small boats rowed across the water underneath the bridge, disturbing the otherwise still reflection of the horse-head gable of a nearby building. A scene like this is said to be typical of ancient Songjiang, little changed since the Ming and Qing dynasties. But the town's history can be traced back even as far as the Spring and Autumn Period (770-476 B.C.).

Old Huating

In the Tang Dynasty, the east end of the Yangtse River Delta was guarded by an embankment. The sites of the present-day Bund and Pudong were still submerged by water. Songjiang was already an important and thriving southeastern town at that time. It was known as Huating. In the Spring and Autumn Period, Huating formed the eastern tip of the territory of the State of Wu, visited by the King of Wu on his hunting trips. The Huating hunting lodge had been built for this purpose. The town assumed military importance due to its nearness to the sea. It was administered as a town during the Sui Dynasty (581-618). Historic relics of one sort or another can be seen today, which testify to these facts.

Walking through the streets and byways of Songjiang, we came to a primary school. In the middle of its playground stands a stone pillar inscribed with scriptures dating back to the Tang Dynasty (618-907). This is perhaps the most ancient architecture in Shanghai. The pillar is over nine meters high. The main body is octagonal in shape, inscribed with scripture, coiled dragons, lions, over ten Buddhist statues, Bodhisattvas and a picture of donors making their offerings. The sculptured statues are

Alleyways in water and an ancient bridge — a typical scene in Songjiang.

This stone pillar inscribed with scripture has stood in Songjiang for over one thousand years. It testifies to the prosperity of Songjiang in the ancient Tang Dynasty.

robust and vivid, the technique mature and style succinct, very much in common with the style of relief found in Tang Dynasty grottoes of the Central Plains.

Stone scripture pillars were introduced to China by the Esoteric Sect of Buddhism during the early Tang Dynasty. According to a Buddhist sutra, pillars should be built to avoid calamity and obtain pardon for sinners. Built at a crossroad near the former office of the county keeper of records, it was where convicts receiving death sentences were executed each autumn. The pillar was intended as a place where the convict might pray to be expiated of sins and be reincarnated. Many such pillars were said to have been built in Huating in the Tang Dynasty. Judging from the number of pillars built and the superb skill with which they were built, Songjiang must have been a town with a sound economy and developed culture even in the early days.

Songjiang Quadrilateral Pagoda

To the east of the Tang Dynasty stone pillar carved with scripture lies an architectural complex of the Song, Yuan, Ming and Qing dynasties. It was an ancient Songjiang quadrilateral pagoda, 48 metres high, that we came to. Before Shanghai developed as a port city this was the highest architecture within a radius of 100 kilometres, and one of the few wooden structures preserved in good condition to date out of many stone-wooden pagodas in the Yangtse River Delta. In front of the pagoda stands a high and massive stone screen wall with a fabulous animal called *tan*, carved in relief, which stood on treasures of silver, coral and jade. According to legend, the animal once enjoyed the wealth of man — gold, silver and treasures — but was so covetous that it even wanted to swallow the sun. The result was that the animal perished in the sea, as it attempted to swallow the sun. Built in 1370, the screen wall advises people not to be

In the Mansion of the Mademoiselle a girl can see opera without leaving her mansion — a privilege enjoyed by the rich.

Mosque in Songjiang surrounded by a dragon wall. It embodies the style of Yuan, Ming and Qing architectures.

greedy like the *tan*. It was formerly part of the Songjiang City God Temple, which was destroyed during war. The wall is the only thing that remains intact, since it is built of stone and bricks. Nearby we found other structures belonging to the Ming and Qing dynasties.

Luxurious Gardens of Former Dynasties

Songjiang was in its heyday in the Ming and Qing dynasties, when the city's industry and commerce thrived. It had the reputation of being a city where the wealth of the nation was concentrated and where business magnates and high-ranking officials lived. A great many gardens were built by the rich merchants and gentlemen. The most famous among them is Zuibaichi, (Pool where Bai became intoxicated). This name refers to the life-style of the famous Tang Dynasty poet, Bai Juyi.

It was said that Bai used to drink wine with his associates on the bank of a pool, singing poetry together. Bai intoxicated himself and sought pleasure this way in his later years. Out of admiration for the poet and in emulation, Han Qi, a prime minster of the Northern Song Dynasty, built

Wife of the deputy imam of the mosque has home furniture that combines Islamic style with the flavour of the people south of the Yangtse. The wife, of course, is a Moslem.

The hall in the mosque has Yuan architectural style side by side with Islamic style.

Zuibaitang (Pavilion where Bai became intoxicated) in the middle of a pond in his own garden. Gu Dashen, a rich merchant of the early Qing Dynasty later built Zuibaichi out of admiration for the famous poet and for the graceful living style of Han Qi.

From Zuibaichi we walked across to another ancient mansion, called Xiaojielou or Mansion of the Mademoiselle. A wealthy merchant built the mansion so his daughter could watch local opera of which she was particularly keen. Since girls were kept in inner apartments and could not go out into the street to see the opera, the two-storey structure was built in such a way that the girl could see the opera being played across the street while keeping herself unseen by others.

We next saw an Islamic mosque in a place in Songjiang called Digangfahang. The enclosure of the mosque is paved with black tiles in the shape of a dragon. In wave-like manner the dragon extends itself along the wall. The main building is higher than the wall. The mosque is said to be one of the oldest extant in China. The sculpture is the same as those seen in Chinese temples, but it is side by side with Islamic architecture in solemness. We were particularly attracted by the hall which serves as the place of worship for Moslems. It has an arched ceiling in Islamic style, with no beams whatsoever. The ceiling looks a very sturdy structure in typical Yuan Dynasty (1271-1368) art form.

How is it that an ancient and exquisite mosque is found in the Yangtse River Delta, where there are not too many Moslems? The reason for this is that in 1277 Songjiang became a prefecture under the Yuan Dynasty. The city which assumed its high position was visited by Mongolians, Huis and people from the Western Regions and Western Xia regime who believed in Islam. The mosque was built for these people. Considering the wealth and the high architectural technique possessed by Songjiang, it was not difficult to build such a mosque in fine style and on such a grand scale.

Translated by He Fei

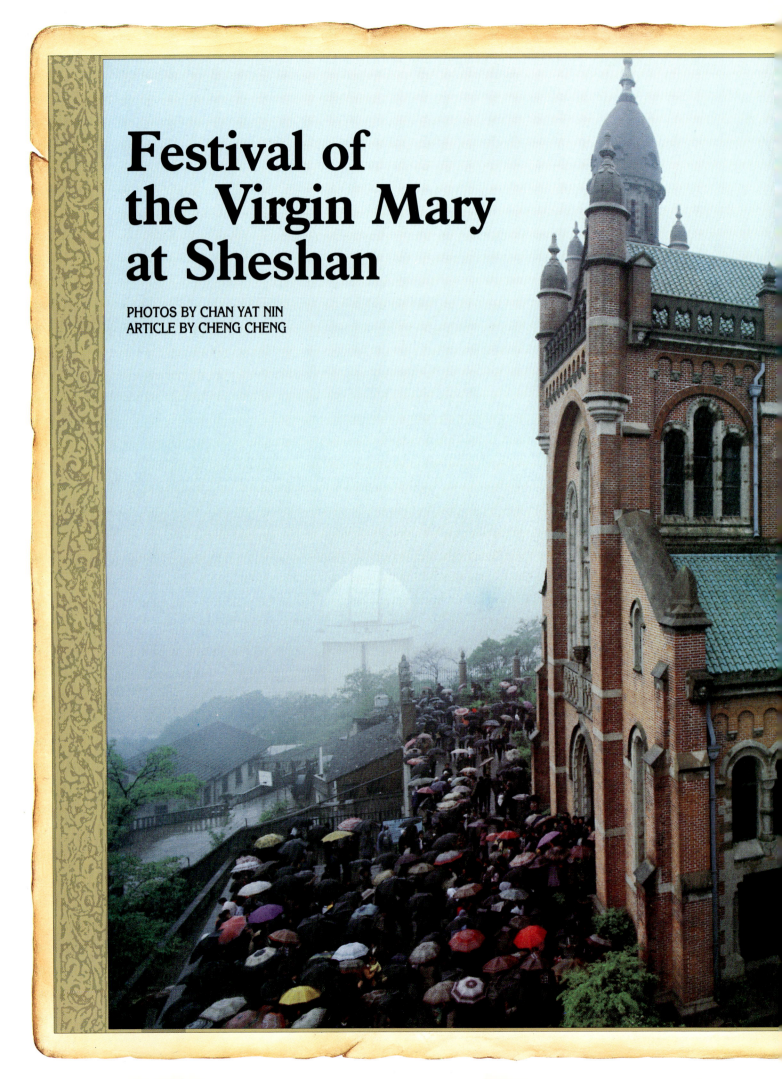

Festival of the Virgin Mary at Sheshan

PHOTOS BY CHAN YAT NIN
ARTICLE BY CHENG CHENG

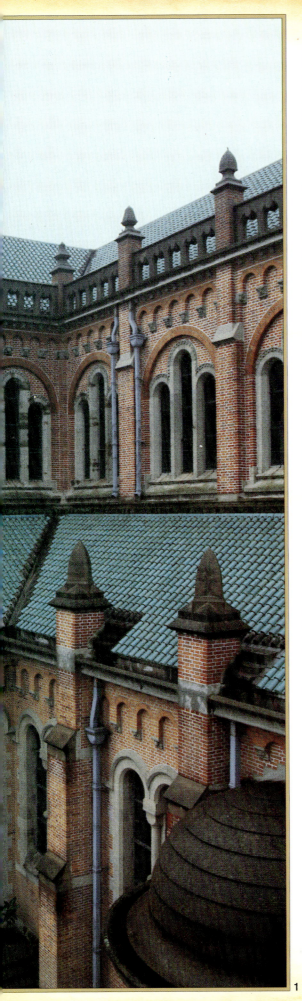

The imposing red-brick church on Sheshan Hill (1) draws thousands of Catholics during the festival month (2). The Bishop of Shanghai arrives on the first day (3) and the choir fills the nave with hymns (4) (last two by Er Dongqiang).

Spring comes to Shanghai in April and May, when Sheshan Hill, renowned since early times, makes a lovely target for an excursion. What really prompted me to visit Sheshan, however, was the famous pilgrimage which takes place to the Catholic church there every May, Our Lady's month, dedicated to the Virgin Mary.

I set off with friends before dawn on the first of May. The road was almost empty of traffic. The cool morning air soon had me wide awake. The light spread across the fields, trees and grass as we passed through what seemed like an endless green belt in the suburbs of Shanghai. We drove for about an hour on a more or less flat road before a small hill appeared. This was Sheshan, thirty-six kilometres from Shanghai's southwestern district of Xujiahui. Some hundred metres high and a magnet for people practising rock-climbing

Today, it is no Buddhist monastery that towers on the hilltop, but the Catholic church known as 'Our Lady of China'. More than half of its red-brick facade is taken up by the main portal and windows. The belfry to the west seems to lift the whole building towards the sky — a sublime and imposing sight, somehow humbling the viewer.

It started to drizzle and our car was forced to slow down as it started up the hill. There did not seem to be anybody else about. 'Too early', I thought to myself. But when we reached the top of the hill, I was surprised to be confronted by a sea of umbrellas. The motor road climbed up by a route which concealed the innumerable paths along which devotees streamed.

In fact, the rain notwithstanding, pilgrims were converging on the church from all directions. The peak pilgrimage times are said to be the very beginning of May,

people attending Mass that first morning of the festival.

Sacred music rang out through the church, played on the pipe organ. The Bishop of Shanghai appeared in his red robes. Several Masses are celebrated in the church during Our Lady's month, but only the opening one is officiated over by the bishop himself. I noted that the nave was supported by twenty massive marble pillars; the distance from floor to roof must be at least thirty meters. With its rounded arches, the church looks almost Romanesque in inspiration. In the light provided by both electricity and candles, the choir at the back started to sing hymns, their music somehow bringing out the contrasting quietness which reigned in the body of the church. Prayers and readings from the Bible followed, led by the bishop. I couldn't understand a word of what was said, however; despite the fact that the Chinese

techniques, Sheshan is considered 'high' in the context of Shanghai, where the average height above sea-level is not even four metres!

Once a sacred place of Buddhism, Sheshan came under attack at three different periods of history — during the Yuan (1271-1368) and early Qing (1644-1911) dynasties and later in the Qing dynasty at the time of the Taiping Heavenly Kingdom (1851-1864) — which virtually wiped out all its Buddhist buildings.

the seventeenth, the twenty-fourth, and then again at the end of the month, and tens of thousands of Catholics come here in the course of the month.

It was a struggle to get into the church through the eager but reverential crowds. It was almost eight o'clock by the time I managed to make my way inside. Mass was about to begin. The scores of rows of pews in the nave were already packed, and there was hardly any standing room in the aisles either. There must have been at least three thousand

Catholic Church has been formally independent from the Vatican since 1957, the Mass in China is still performed in Latin.

The mixed congregation listened intently with lowered heads and closed eyes. On an upper balcony a group of village women knelt, reciting a prayer with fervour. The bishop blessed wafers and wine in the usual way and a file of people went forward to kneel at the altar steps and take communion. Some kissed the bishop's ring in reverence as they accepted the wafer.

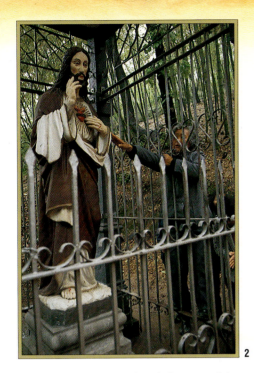

After the service had ended, many of the gathering went to await their turn at the confessional. Those who had been unable to get into the church for the Mass now also seized the opportunity to crowd in.

I went out to investigate the path which runs around the hill roughly half-way up. I had noticed many of the pilgrims arriving via this path earlier, so I decided to take it on my way downhill. Sheshan Hill is not steep, but the path winds up and down on itself in a real zigzag. Its route is symbolic of the *via dolorosa*, the path taken by Jesus Christ as he was condemned to death, crowned with the cruel crown of thorns, nailed to the cross and flogged as he carried it on his back to the site of the Crucifixion. For the Catholic worshippers, it is an integral part of their pilgrimage to trace the fourteen 'stations of the Cross', as they are called. In so doing they atone for their misdeeds and empathize with Christ in his travails. I saw many family groups of all ages and entire villages who had travelled to Sheshan as a group, with identification badges on their chests. Some even carried flags with the village name on them to help them keep together — that's how many people were there! There were a lot of children who seemed very well-behaved, following their elders and betters as they made their way along the still wet path (the rain had in the meantime stopped).

I walked downhill against the flow of pilgrims, so I was able to gauge the full extent of their rather solemn mood. They sang hymns as they walked, deepening the religious atmosphere on the hillside. Whenever they came to a shrine, a 'station of the cross', containing a statue illustrating one of the different stages on Christ's route, they knelt, ignoring the mud, some reading from the prayer books or Bible they carried with them.

The pilgrims' circuit starts at Zhongshan Hall, halfway up the hill. Opposite the hall there is a pavilion containing images of the Holy Family — Mary, Joseph and the Infant Jesus — which always has a group of devotees standing around it. Hundreds of candles burn around the Virgin Mary, reflecting their glow on the faces of the kneeling believers.

This pilgrimage to Sheshan during Our Lady's month has been a major event for Catholics south of the River Yangtse for some time. The Catholic Church went through very difficult times in China in the nineteenth century. In 1870, for example, during a wave of xenophobia, a Catholic church in Tianjin was burnt down after rumours spread that the foreign missionaries were abducting Chinese children and instigating crimes. In Shanghai, too, where Christianity had existed since the

Ming dynasty when Xu Guangqi became a disciple of the famous Jesuit Matteo Ricci (1550-1610), this was a disturbingly volatile period. In 1863 a few single-storey buildings, one of them a chapel, had been erected on the southern slope of Sheshan by the Catholic Church of Shanghai. A French missionary added a hexagonal pavilion with a large iron cross on top in 1867 which drew Catholics from all around to worship. The acting bishop of the Shanghai diocese thus decided to seek shelter at Sheshan, promising the Virgin Mary that he would build a bigger and better church if she would grant him protection. And, indeed, in 1873 he was able to redeem his pledge. On completion of the new church, the ecclesiastical authorities fixed the first Sunday in May as the date on which to celebrate the event, and the pilgrimage started in earnest.

At the foot of the hill I came upon a narrow stream choked with fishing boats, some of them containing pictures of the Holy Family, the Trinity, and so on. These act to remind them of their pilgrimage and are replaced each year. Some of the boat-dwellers had hoisted a flag emblazoned with a cross to identify themselves as Christian pilgrims. Most of the floating population in the Shanghai area are Catholics, I was told, and some families have professed the faith for generations. During the 'cultural revolution', all religious activities were banned and church property was confiscated. However, it has been reported that more than twenty churches have opened again in Shanghai since 1980.

I was eager to find out more about the link between the fisherfolk and Catholicism. In the old days, I was told, they lived a life of hardship and found solace in this religion. When they had to move to another place in the search for better fishing grounds, they would leave their children with the Catholic community at Sheshan. The children were subsequently given an education and were influenced by religion from an early age. They tended to grow up to be pious Catholics. Although many of the fisherfolk have left their boats to make a living ashore in recent years, they still come to Sheshan every year without fail to pay homage to the Virgin Mary. Other worshippers come from other parts of the Shanghai municipality, from neighbouring Jiangsu and Zhejiang, and even from far-off Guangdong, Shangdong, Shaanxi and Inner Mongolia. This flocking to Sheshan in Our Lady's month has become part of the social framework handed down from generation to generation, rather like the annual pilgrimage undertaken by fishermen on the south coast of China to invoke the protection of Tianhou, the patron goddess of seafarers.

Translated by He Fei

The devout pack into the lofty nave (1), receiving communion (4) and queuing to make their confession (3) before setting out on a circuit of the shrines (2).

Village pilgrims immerse themselves in prayer (1), then pray at each of the 'stations of the Cross' on the hill (2, by Er Dongqiang, and 5). Many of the fishing boats moored below Sheshan Hill (4) have a religious picture in the place of honour (3).

A Garden in the Land of Waters

PHOTOS BY CHAN YAT NIN   ARTICLE BY SHENG ZHI

In a misty area of the Yangtse Valley there stands a cluster of buildings modelled on the fictional Qing-dynasty residential complex Grand View Garden, described in the classic Chinese novel *A Dream of Red Mansions*, which has been justly popular for over two hundred years.

Willows sway in the breeze just like they do in the novel, but the upturned eaves and the grass dotted with yellow flowers know nothing of the unhappy fate of the novel's characters. This Grand View Garden is far from its original setting in the imperial capital, Beijing; instead it stands by reed-clogged Lake Dianshan on the outskirts of Shanghai in southeastern China.

Why in the South?

In the novel, Daguanyuan or Grand View Garden was located in Beijing and indeed the capital does now itself have a similar complex (see CHINA TOURISM no. 86). But Shanghai also boasts a Grand View Garden, which was not built south of the River Yangtse without justification.

Firstly, the author of the novel — Cao Xueqin (?–1763) — was born and spent his childhood not so far to the northwest in Nanjing, Jiangsu Province. Secondly, according to historical records, the author's great-grandfather Cao Xi moved south from Beijing in 1663 and was appointed the Textile Commissioner of Jiangning Prefecture. There the Cao family stayed and prospered until, in 1728, Cao Xueqin's father Cao Fu having lost favour with Emperor Yongzheng, was removed from his official post. The family estates were confiscated and they were forced to move back to Beijing.

Occupying an area of 106.7 hectares, this Grand View Garden stands beside Lake Dianshan in Qingpu County, some sixty-five kilometres southwest of Shanghai's city centre. The trip takes about two hours by car through countryside dotted with villages of whitewashed houses set in clumps of bamboo, plum trees, peach trees and so on. Often there is a rivulet flowing by in front, and the houses are reflected in the water.

From the small bridge at which vehicles stop, it is a good idea to climb the nearby pagoda, a replica of an ancient tower. From here there is a bird's-eye view of Grand View Garden below, surrounded by the sparkling waters of Lake Dianshan. The buildings are set among luxuriant vegetation in a style typical of gardens south of the Yangtse. A white wall at the foot of the pagoda extends to the lakeside. Small boats ply the watercourses crisscrossing the fields around.

The Twelve Beauties of Jinling

I followed the zigzags of the tree-shaded path until it reached a stone archway on the lintel of which was inscribed 'Illusory Land of Great Void'. On either side stood a couplet; together the two read: 'When false is taken for true, true becomes false. If non-being turns into being, being becomes non-being.' This, I believe, is the underlying message of the novel, which chronicles the gradual downfall of an aristocratic family as it squanders its fortune.

Beyond the archway stands a large screen wall, its granite facade carved in bold relief. At the top left you can identify the goddess Nüwa (sister and consort of Fuxi, the legendary ancestor of the humun race) who, according to fable, melted down rocks to repair the vault of heaven when it collapsed. She is shown casting a piece of rock right into the centre of this screen wall. On the rock is carved a handsome boy — the spoilt yet sensitive hero of the novel, Jia Baoyu. The back of the screen wall is inlaid with a white marble slab depicting the 'Twelve Beauties of Jinling', the leading female characters in the novel, each as beautiful as a fairy.

Screen walls shield the entrance to an imposing residence, temple or hall, not only to preserve the privacy of those inside but also to make it more difficult for evil spirits to enter, since it was said that these could

only move in a straight line. Such screens are a common feature in the south. However, no such thing is described in the Grand View Garden of the novel. Apart from this, elements like the *dougong* brackets and the openwork bricks are all typical of the southern school of garden landscaping, the most famous examples of which are to be found in Jiangsu's Suzhou.

White Walls and Black Tiles

Behind the screen wall stands the main entrance to Grand View Garden. Once inside, you see a cluster of buildings in the same southern style, with whitewashed walls and jet-black roof tiles. The lintel above each door is meticulously carved. At first glance, the contrast between the black and white is very strong. However, there is no clash; the colours complement each other beautifully. Some of the windows have individual black-tiled eaves built out over them for protection.

Passing through the heavy red gate you come to a group of rocks of strange and wonderful forms covered with moss. I strolled along the zigzag path between and came to a moon gate made of slit bamboo stems. This is the entrance to Yihongyuan (Happy Red Court), the home of Jia Baoyu. Behind the white wall there is a small pond flanked by more rockeries and weeping willows. Dotted around the courtyard of the house are bananas, crab-apples, full-bloomed Chinese trumpet creepers and many other trees and plants. It is all rather romantic, and yet Baoyu turned his back on it and became a priest after he was tricked into marrying a different woman than his beloved Lin Daiyu.

Next along the path is Longcui'an (Green Lattice Nunnery), where the lay nun Miaoyu, one of the Twelve Beauties, steeped herself in Buddhism. Full of trees and flowers, it is quiet and clean, intended perhaps to reflect Miaoyu's obsession with cleanliness. Though not very large, the nunnery contains a combined drum and bell tower, a cell for meditation and rooms for other purposes. The yellow walls and black roof reflect the traditions of the south again as regards Buddhist structures. Outside, the smoke of burning joss-sticks lingers in the air above the huge incense-burner.

Homes of Two Heroines

Hengwuyuan (Alpinia Park) and Xiaoxiangguan (Bamboo Lodge) are set very close together as if the designer deliberately wanted to underline the comparison between their respective inhabitants, Xue Baochai and Lin Daiyu.

The first thing you see inside Alpinia Park are huge rocks and a tiny stream whose waters flow past the pavilion on its banks and into a lotus pond. Banana leaves quiver in the breeze. From upstairs in the main building, you have a superb view over the interior courtyard, with a long covered corridor amidst flowers and greenery. Maybe the design indicates Xue Baochai's reserved, calculating nature. However, instead of being furnished simply and plainly as in the novel, her rooms here are elaborate, perhaps to emphasize that this distant cousin of the Jias came from a rich family. She it was who eventually married Jia Baoyu only to lose him.

By way of contrast, Bamboo Lodge is decorated in a manner faithful to the original, simply, but with elegance and taste. The house is surrounded by clumps of bamboos and the whole place seems to lurk under a green shade. In

Grand View Garden on the banks of Lake Dianshan (2) is fronted by a screen wall depicting the 'Twelve Beauties of Jinling' in white marble (1).

the courtyard, there is a rivulet with a small arched stone bridge over it. The furniture — tables, chairs, bed, bookcases and so on — in Lin Daiyu's home are all made of good solid wood in the southern style. Yet they look as though they are made of bamboo, a plant which the intelligent, pensive girl loved. Very noticeable is the large earthenware pot for brewing herbal medicines set beside the bed, reminding us of Lin Daiyu's frail health. Eventually, she dies of a broken heart, her love for her cousin Jia Baoyu thwarted by the machinations of other family members.

Throne for an Imperial Concubine

Next you should go and see Grand View Pavilion, the major building in the garden complex. In front there is a pond surrounded by white jade balustrades, with a white marble archway inscribed with characters reading 'House of Reunion'. In the novel Jia Zheng, the head of the family, spends all the revenue accumulated over several generations on building the House of Reunion purely for his eldest daughter, the imperial concubine Yuanchun, to come to visit her parents on a single occasion on the evening of the Lantern Festival. The author Cao Xueqin described it like this: '... it was wreathed with the perfumed smoke of incense, splendid with flowers, brilliant with countless lanterns, melodious with strains of soft music. Words fail to describe the scene of peaceful magnificence and noble refinement.'

Grand View Pavilion, where the imperial concubine receives all the members of the Rong and Ning households of the Jia family, is roomy and bright. A throne is set in the

centre of the hall as befits her imperial status. A red carpet leads from the floor level to the throne, something again which is normally only seen in a palace.

From the top floor of the Grand View Pavilion, you have a panoramic view over the entire garden and beyond. The buildings close at hand are the highest and most magnificent. Since yellow was the colour reserved for the emperor, green for his wives and concubines, the roofs of Grand View Pavilion are covered with green glazed tiles. Otherwise, all the other buildings visible have black roofs. Set in amongst the thick foliage, the white walls and black roofs merge to form a harmonious traditional image typical of the regions south of the Yangtse. The misty scene has a fittingly timeless appeal....

Translated by Wang Mingjie

Elements typical of traditional buildings south of the Yangtse: roof and gable ornamentation (1), exaggeratedly upcurved eaves (4), and window eaves (5). Happy Red Court, with its small pond

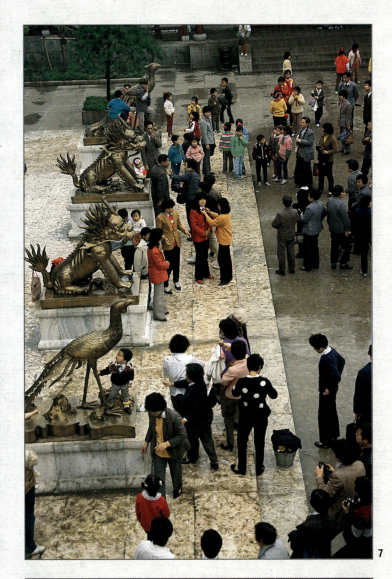

(3) and mandarin ducks (2). The bedchamber of the frail Lin Daiyu (6). Unicorn and phoenix (7) lead up to Grand View Pavilion, containing the imperial concubine's throne (9). Archway emblazoned with 'House of Reunion' (8).

Tourist Guide to Shanghai

Contents

Tourist Map of Shanghai	**90**
What to See in Shanghai ?	**92**
Treasure-Hunting in Shanghai/Shanghai's Family Museums and Exhibition Houses	**98**
Major Scenic Spots	**99**
Administrative Organizations Related to Foreign Affairs/ Major Travel Agencies	**100**
Major Recreational Centres	**101**
Star-Rated Hotels/Climatic Conditions in Shanghai	**102**
Major Restaurants	**103**
Major Shopping Centres	**104**
Major Transportation Companies	**105**

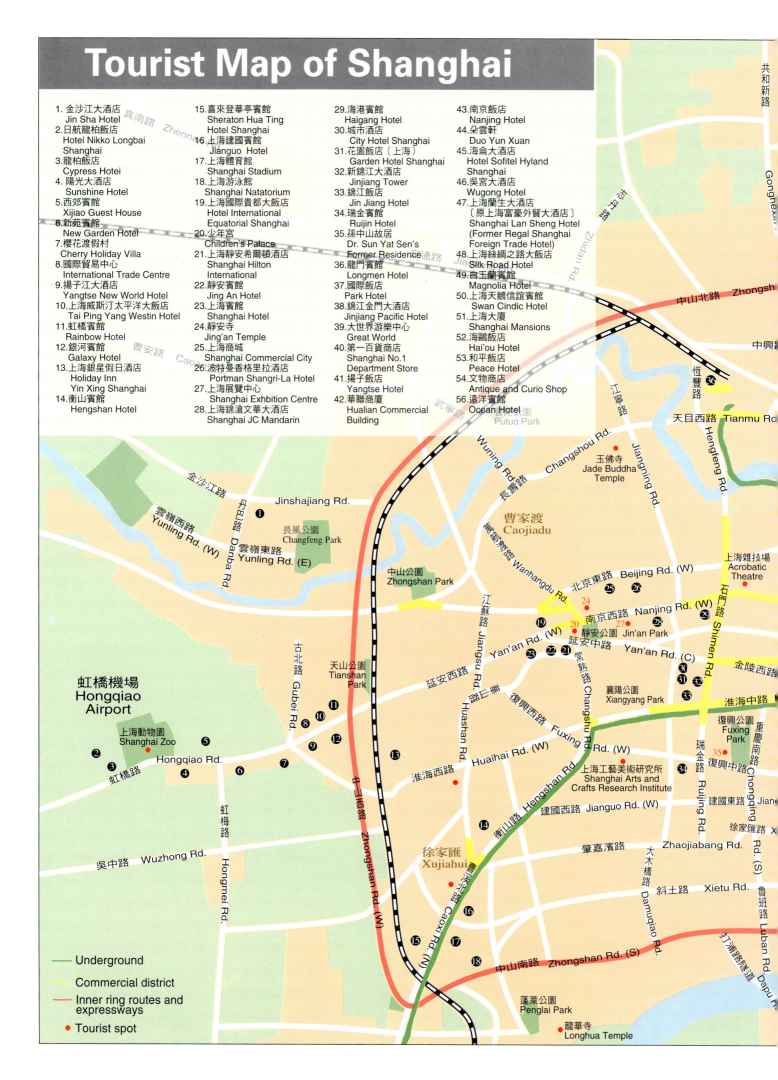

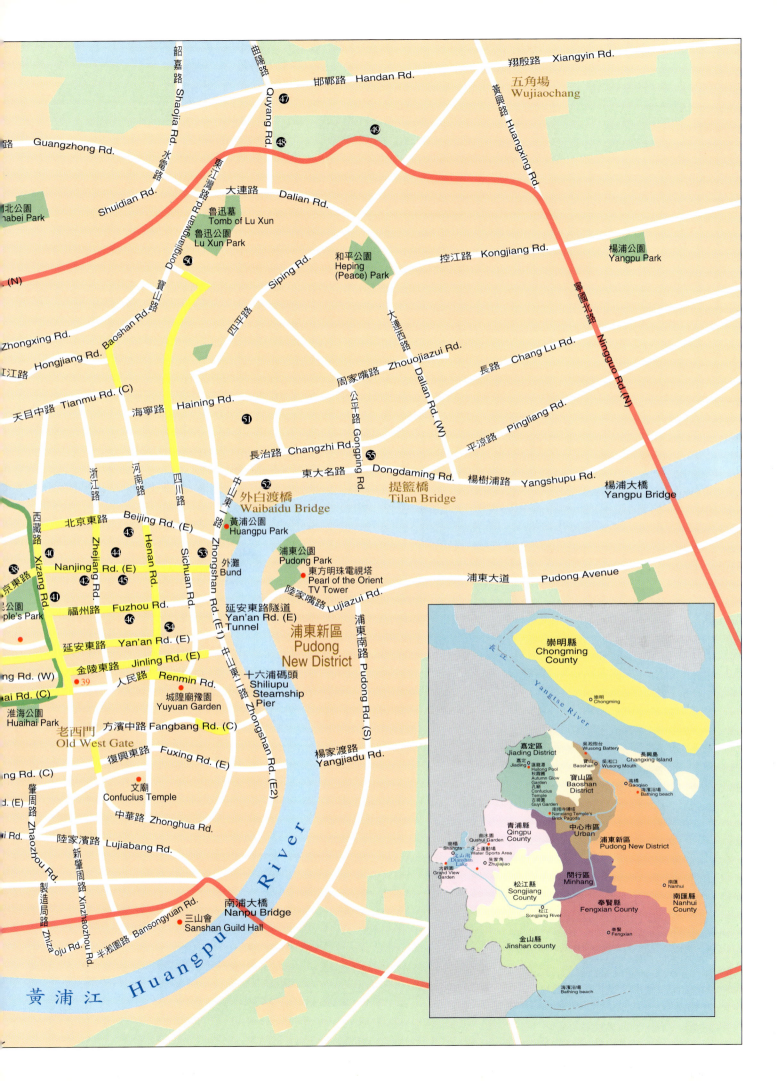

What to See in Shanghai?

ARTICLE BY CHAN YAT NIN & SHU YUANCHENG

There is a saying among tourists in China which goes: Go to Xi'an if you want to see things 2,000 years old; go to Beijing if you want to see things 1,000 years old; and go to Shanghai if you want to see things of the last hundred years.

In Shanghai, there are several hundred buildings that bear witness to the architectural styles of the last hundred years, and which have given the great metropolis the reputation of being a "museum of international architecture". Here you can also find a culture and romanticism that combines both traditional Chinese and Western elements — a physical product of the last hundred years. You can see ancient sites that already existed before Shanghai became a city, and which seemed all the more valuable after the ups and downs in the foreign settlements. The suburban counties and districts feature some tourist attractions different from those in the urban areas: the villages and lakes and canals which have a history longer than that of urban Shanghai.

Shanghai's Geographical Features

Administratively speaking, Shanghai is the largest of the three municipalities directly under the Central Government. The total area of Shanghai is 6,186 square kilometres, of which 351 square kilometres are the urban districts, a region still growing. The total population is 12.62 million, and seven million live in urban districts.

Situated on the southern bank of the Yangtse River's mouth and looking across the East China Sea, Shanghai stands on the alluvial plain of the Yangtse River Delta. This piece of very flat land is crisscrossed with waterways. The weather is mild and damp and the four seasons are highly distinct. The Huangpu River, a major waterway of the city, cuts Shanghai into two parts, the east and the west. It is in the western part that stands the centre of town.

1. The area embracing the City God's Temple is the most traditional commercial centre in Shanghai (by Ma Yuanhao).

2. The Mid-Lake Pavilion at Yuyuan Garden is a typical of southern Chinese architecture (by Chan Yat Nin).

3. The Confucius Temple in Shanghai has become a recreation site (by Chan Yat Nin).

4. A view from the Shanghai Mansion: On the left spanning the Suzhou River is the Waibai Ferry Bridge. On the right is the sluice bridge recently built at Wusong Road (by Liu Bingyuan).

5. The former residence of Sun Yat-sen is still arranged as it was (by Tao Hongxing).

6. The Mose Guild Hall in Hongkou District was a meeting place for the Jews living in Shanghai during World War II (by Xie Guanghui).

Besides the urban districts, Jiading District, Songjiang and Qingpu counties in rural Shanghai are the richest in tourist resources. Since Shanghai is so large and complicated, how does one tour the city? The following introduction is meant to satisfy tourists with different interests.

The International Architectural Museum Tour

Shanghai boasts more than 300 Western-style residential houses, public buildings, commercial structures and religious centres from different historical periods. They not only reflect Western architectural features in different periods, but also the particular styles of different Western countries and nationalities. Most of the public and commercial buildings cluster in Huangpu District in the eastern part of the city, while both Chinese and Western residential houses of various styles concentrate in the quiet districts of Jing'an, Luwan and Xuhui. This leads to three tourist routes.

A Walking Tour

The tour begins from the riverside area known as The Bund and tourists may have breakfast at the Sea Gull Hotel, north of the Waibai Ferry Bridge. Then they may go to the top of the hotel to have a panoramic view of the Huangpu River in the morning. From here, they will see dozens of Western-style buildings stretching along the Huangpu and Suzhou rivers merging below.

From the latter half of the 19th century to the first half of the 20th, the Bund area was the heart of the foreign financial and monetary institutions. From 1848, several dozen banks from Britain, France, the United States, Russia, Germany, Japan, Holland and Belgium had their offices along one side of the street across the road from the river.

Along the riverside are buildings representing the early colonial architecture (the former British consulate and now the Shanghai Foreign Trade Bureau); the Renaissance-imitation architecture (the south building of the Peace Hotel which was formerly called Huizhong Hotel); modern international architecture (Shanghai Mansion); modern US architecture of the Chicago School (Sassoon House, now the North Building of the Peace Hotel) and Greek architecture, featuring the use of huge pillars (the portico of the Customs House building). The most eye-catching is the building of the Shanghai and Hong Kong Banking Corporation, rebuilt in 1921, which now serves as the office of the People's Government of Shanghai. With a combination of Renaissance and Greek styles, it was one of the most elegant buildings in the Far East.

From 7:30 to 10:00 (time may vary from season to season) every evening, buildings along the Bund, cast in coloured lights, appear all the more elegant.

Bicycle Tour

Xuhui, Luwan and Jing'an districts in the western part of Shanghai were originally inhabited by foreigners and rich Chinese. In these areas are predominantly Spanish garden houses. In addition, there are French, Italian and British villas. The best way to go and see these romantic buildings is to rent a bike, and ride leisurely under the shade of Chinese parasol trees.

Typical buildings include the Jinjiang Club representing Renaissance and French classical architecture; the Russian East Orthodox Church in Xiangyang Park on Huaihai Road; the Verdun Garden, 39-45 South Shaanxi Road, representing European residences, the China Painting Institute on Yueyang Road representing Italian villas; Spanish style houses on Wuxing and Hengshan roads; the Veteran Cadres Bureau on Yueyang Road representing German residential buildings; the Huaye Building on North Shaanxi Road representing multi-storey Spanish houses; buildings typical of British country houses along the Hongqiao Road; official residences of the Renaissance and French classical architectural style as seen at 79 Fengyang Road; and the marble building housing the Children's Palace on Yan'an Road (the former Five-Country Club) in imitation of European palaces.

There are two sites that are not to be missed. One is the magnificent twin-tower Catholic Church at Xujiahui and the other a Norwegian building on Shaanxi Road and Yan'an Road which was the residence of a man called Muller who made his fortune from gambling.

Famous Residence Tour

Often the unusual experiences of the occupants of a house give historical significance to the structure, since so often the story of a house is the story of a person. Shanghai, the site of so many upsurges in modern Chinese history, has been the home of many notable figures. (See the list of residences of notable figures.) A site as a meeting place of foreigners has only been discovered recently at 2 Changyang Road, the Mose Hall for the Jews. First built in 1927, it became a religious centre for the Jews who fled to China before World War II. Now it serves as the History Museum of Jewish Refugees to China and has drawn many visitors of all backgrounds.

The International Architectural Museum Tour may be done in a day and a half for a quick look or may take days to get a close look at the buildings. The suggested normal time for this tour is two to three days.

Former Residences of Shanghai Celebrities in Western Architectural Styles	
Residence of Dr. Sun Yat-sen	1 Xiangshan Road
Residence of Soong Ching Ling (Mme. Sun Yat-sen)	Huaihai Road Central
Residence of Lu Xun (great Chinese writer)	9 Dalu Xincun, Shanyin Road
Residence of Zhou En-lai (the late Premier)	73 Ennan Road
Residence of Chiang Kai-shek	9 Dongping Road
Residence of T.V. Soong	145 Yueyang Road
Residence of Cai Yuanpei	16 Lane 303, Huashan Road
Residence of Bai Chongxi	150 Fenyang Road
Residence of George C. Marshall	160 Taiyuan Road
Private Mansion of Ellis Kadoorie	Municipal Children's Palace
Sassoon House	Peace Hotel, 20 Nanjing Road East
Hardoo's Private Mansion	Meili Garden, Tongren Road
Residence of Du Yuesheng	Dongyu Guesthouse, Donghu Road
Residence of Huang Jinrong	Guilin Park

Shanghai Urban Cultural Relics Tour

Shanghai is not just a metropolitan famous for its prosperous commerce, it is also abundant with high-class cultural relics and historical sites. A look at the cultural relics and historical attractions may be done in two different ways.

SHANGHAI CITY MAP

The Old Town of Shanghai

Once you have set foot on Renmin Road, you are already in the territory of the old Shanghai County seat. The circle formed by Renmin Road and Zhonghua Road was where the old city wall used to stand, and inside the circle was the old town. The city wall has been replaced by roads, but some of the former structures inside the old town still stand.

The most well-known are the Yuyuan Garden and the City God's Temple which, standing next to each other, are all in the northeastcorner of the old town of Shanghai. The people in Shanghai customarily use the name of the City God's Temple for both places. Trolley buses Nos. 11, 16 and 26 and buses Nos. 64 and 66 take visitors to Laobeimen or the Old North Gate from where visitors walk southward to reach the place.

The best time to be at the City God's Temple is between seven or eight in the morning in order to try at the delicacies of a traditional breakfast. Then the visitor may walk over the Nine-Twist Bridge to have tea at the Mid-Lake Pavilion located in a lotus pond. The Yuyuan Garden opens at 8:30 and tourists at this time are scarce, giving the interested visitor time and room to have a close look at the place. A private garden owned by Pan Yunduan, Administration Commissioner of Sichuan during the Ming Dynasty, it is over 400 years old. Small and exquisitely built, its sceneries include rockeries, Ten-Thousand Flower Tower, Happy Fish Pavilion, Spring Heralding Tower, Panoramic View Tower, Splendid Jade Hall and Garden Within Garden which combine to present a model of ancient south China classical gardens with a unique grace and tranquil atmosphere. It must be noted that the garden has what's called a garden stabilizing treasure known as the "Exquisite Jade". Actually a rock from Lake Taihu with beautiful holes, it is believed to date back to the Sui (581-618) and Tang (618-907) dynasties. The tour of the garden usually takes about an hour and half.

Once out of the garden, the visitor comes to the City God's Temple. Recently renovated, it once again has become a worshipping ground. By the temple are plenty of shops selling arts and handicrafts including antiques, jade ware, gold and silver jewellry and local produce. Not far from the temple are the Confucius Temple and White Cloud Temple.

Located on Wenmiao Road in southwestern part of the old Shanghai town, the Confucius Temple dates back to the Southern Song Dynasty (1127-1279). Inside the temple are some ancient buildings such as the Dacheng Hall, the Big Dipper Pavilion, the True Ethic Hall and the Scripture Worshipping Pavilion. Built in 1883, the White Cloud Temple on Fangxie Road outside the West Gate of the old Shanghai town is the birth place of the Quanzhen Sect of Taoism in Shanghai. Worshipped in the temple is a statue of the Jade Emperor. Often Taoist activities and ceremonies are held in the temple. Those interested in antiques may go to Dongtai Road outside the West Gate or Fuyou Road inside the North Gate in the old Shanghai town to look for what may catch their fancy. On these two roads, lined with shops featuring antiques, arts and handicrafts, visitors will get a sense of what the collectors' market in Shanghai is like.

Altogether the City God's Temple tour can be completed within a day or even in half a day.

1. *The Jade Buddha statue is a treasure stabilizing the temple at the Jade Buddha Temple (by Tang Zaiqing).*

2. *A Gothic building, the towering Xujiahui Cathedral, gives one a sense of sacredness (by Chan Yat Nin).*

3. *Taoist monks from the White Cloud Temple during a religious ceremony to the accompaniment of Taoist music (by Chan Yat Nin).*

4. *The China St. Mary's Hall on top of Sheshan Hill is one of the most esteemed Catholic holy grounds in China (by Chan Yat Nin).*

94

Religious Attractions Tour

Buddhism has had a long history in Shanghai. In modern history, Shanghai was an important city for the spread of Western religions (Catholicism and Protestantism, for example) in China. Naturally, the place has many temples and churches which tend to concentrate in the western part of the city, giving rise today to a religious attractions tour, which might begin at Longhua Temple, going to Xujiahui Church, Jing'an Church and Jade Buddha Temple.

The Longhua Temple can be reached by taking buses Nos. 41, 44, 56 and 86. Once at the old town of Longhua, the first thing to meet the visitor's eye is the octagonal Longhua Pagoda, 40 metres high with seven storeys. This pavilion type of brick and wood structure is decorated with jingling wind bells on all its eaves. On top of the pagoda, the visitor is rewarded with a view of the high-rises of central Shanghai in the north and the beautiful rural land of south China to the south.

Opposite the pagoda, the Longhua Temple dates back more then 1,750 years. Having experienced prosperity and decay on many occasions, the temple consists of the Hall of the Maitreya Buddha, the Heavenly Kings Hall, the Grand Hall, the Three-Sages Hall, the Hall of Arhats and the towers of bell and drum in Song-dynasty architectural style. Preserved in the temple are a portrait of Sakyamuni after he became a Buddha, more than 7,000 volumes of Buddhist scriptures, a seal bestowed by Emperor Shenzong (r. 1573-1620) of the Ming Dynasty, a gilded two-metre-high bronze statue of Vairocana Buddha and a Thousand-Armed Boddhisattva. Besides this, there are the hundred-year-old peonies and the Longhua Bell which are unique to the temple. On every New Year's Eve, 108 monks and tourists strike the bell to bid goodbye to the old year and usher in the new. In the third month of the lunar calendar, a temple fair is held at Longhua Temple which sees a great fanfare.

Going on Bus No. 44 from the Longhua Temple, one comes to the Catholic church at Xujiahui which once was the largest Catholic parish in China. Xu Guanqi, Shanghai's first Catholic convert and his children, most of whom were Catholics, used to live here. No wonder the place was full of monasteries and convents. The Xujiahui Cathedral, built in 1904, still stands as a centre for Catholics in Shanghai today. The cathedral has two opposite bell towers on the east and west which are over 50 metres high. In the cathedral are 19 altars and a Mass hall large enough for 2,500 worshippers.

To go from the cathedral to the Jing'an Temple, one may take the No. 15 bus and get off at West Nanjing Road. The first ever to go up in Shanghai, the temple is said to have been first built during the Three Kingdoms period (220-280). Repairs in recent years have brought more and more Buddhist believers to come and worship, once again making it a busy Buddhist holy ground. The most valuable object in the temple is the huge bell, cast in 1183, with more than 3,000 kilogrammes of copper. A stone tablet carved with characters in the hand of Song-dynasty Emperor Guangzong (r. 1190-1194) is inlaid in the wall of the temple. As well as the temple fair held on the eighth day of the fourth lunar month, another important Buddhist religious event is the secret teaching session which always attracts a great deal of disciples whenever it occurs.

Devoted Buddhist believers should go and visit the Jade Buddha Temple at Jiangning and Anyuan roads which can be reached by trolley buses Nos. 16, 19 and 24 and buses Nos. 54, 68 and 76. To go from the Jing'an Temple, the No. 76 bus provides the most convenient route.

Right inside a busy downtown district, the Zen temple is small in scale. The Jade Buddha Tower, which is the main structure in the temple, houses two jade Sakyamuni statues brought to the site from Myanmar. The reclining one is about 90 centimetres long and the sitting one is 190 centimetres tall. Both shining jade statues show the Buddha with a kindly expression.

Western Suburb Tour

The two counties of Songjiang and Qingpu and the District of Jiading spread out from south to north, forming the western suburbs of Shanghai. Since they became part of the mainland earlier than the urban districts, they enjoy a longer history. Their rich resources of sites of historical interest, beautiful hills and lakes and a host of modern tourist facilities that have been recently built constitute an ideal area for holiday-making in Shanghai. To see the two counties and one district, the visitor may need to spend two to three days, either by going back to the urban area or staying at the counties for the night.

Songjiang — The County Once Governed Shanghai

Hopping onto a bus at the West Area Bus Depot at 240 North Caobei Road, in southwestern suburban Shanghai, one arrives at Songjiang in under an hour. One of the oldest towns in Shanghai, Songjiang was called Huating County during the reign of Tianbao (742-756) of the Tang Dynasty. It became the site of Songjiang County during the Yuan Dynasty (1271-1368) and its jurisdiction included Shanghai. Today in this ancient town there are many ancient

5. *The Square Pagoda at Songjiang (by Chan Yat Nin)*
6. *The magnificent-looking Grand View Garden by Dianshan Lake (by Chan Yat Nin)*
7. *A barbecue site by Dingshan Lake (by Chan Yat Nin)*

sites, arched bridges over streams and roads paved with stone slabs, typical of a south China town with a long history. The Square Pagoda in the southeast corner of the town is one of the most famous spots of historical interest. The pagoda was first built during the Five Dynasties period (907-960) and rebuilt during the Song Dynasty (960-1279). The square body of this nine-storey and 48.5-metre-high structure give it the name of Square Pagoda. The pagoda we see today is of Song Dynasty architectural style and still contains Song Dynasty murals of the Buddha. Though more than 880 years have passed, the *nan* wood pillars supporting the pagoda are still intact. In the ancient town of Songjiang stands Shanghai's oldest structure — a stone tablet erected in 895, carved with the complete text of the Dharani Sutra. The tablet is 9.3 metres high with 21 tiers. Apart from the scripture, also carved are Buddhist images of elephants, lions and waves.

After visiting Songjiang, the visitor may go, along the Husong Highway, to Sheshan Hill, on top of which stands the China St. Mary's Hall. A Catholic church, the place hosts a grand ceremony in memory of the Virgin Mary every May and thousands of people of Catholic faith from neighbouring provinces come to take part in the event.

Dianshan Lake in Qingpu — Shanghai's Largest Scenic Area

A dozen kilometres west of Sheshan Hill is the boundary of Qingpu County, which, amongst other things, is known for the Songze and Fuquan Hill ancient cultural sites dating from the Neolithic Age to the Western Zhou (c. 11th century-770 B.C.). The Grand View Garden and Fork Club and other tourist attractions built at the Dianshan Lake Scenic Area have made the place very attractive to tourists in Shanghai. The county seat, 42 kilometres from Shanghai's urban districts is an ancient town embraced by water on all four sides.

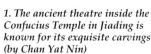

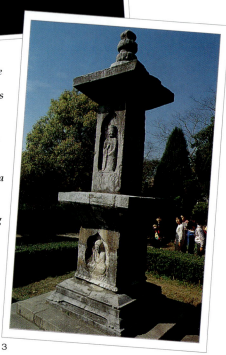

The Qushui (Crooked Water) Garden in the northeastern part of the town is one of the most famous gardens in Shanghai. Erected in 1745, the garden was built with a lake at its centre. Such structures as the Sunlight Greeting Pavilion, Happy Rain Bridge, Moonlight Pavilion and Sunset Tower, connected by long corridors and embellished with rockeries, aged pines and vines, spread along the lakeside. It is indeed a quiet and beautiful spot.

Eight kilometres west of the county seat of Qingpu is another ancient town called Zhujiajiao, known for its water town scenery typical in regions south of the Yangtse River. The streets here are lined up with ancient-style shops and on the river bank are residential houses in the Qing-dynasty architectural style. The Setting-the-Fish-Free Bridge built in the Ming Dynasty (1368-1644) is the oldest bridge in Shanghai.

Dianshan Lake is west of Zhujiajiao Town. From the town, buses running on the Qingpu-Shangta Road drive for a dozen kilometres until they pull in at the last stop at Shangta, the centre of the Dianshan Lake Scenic Area. There are also buses

1. The ancient theatre inside the Confucius Temple in Jiading is known for its exquisite carvings (by Chan Yat Nin)

2. Elegant little pottery figures decorate the roof-top of the Main Hall at the Confucius Temple in Jiading (by Chan Yat Nin).

3. A Song-dynasty stone pagoda in the Autumn Glow Garden

4. It is most exciting to ride on the roller-coaster at the Jinjiang Amusement Park (by Xie Guanghui).

5. The Great World is a nightclub for the common folk of Shanghai (by Xie Guanghui).

6. It is a novel experience to watch equine contests at the Jinjiang Amusement Park (by Xie Guanghui).

7. The inner decoration of the famous Western restaurant, the Red House (by Tang Zaiqing)

going from Shanghai city proper to this stop and the entire distance is 64 kilometres. The largest scenic area in suburban Shanghai, it features a water sports park, swimming pools, camping sites, the Grand View Garden, a golf course, etc. Built according to descriptions in the classical novel *A Dream of Red Mansions*, the Grand View Garden consists of three groups of architecture: the Yihong Courtyard, Xiaoxiang Residence and Xiurenmude Hall, including the Grand View Tower, Hengwu Courtyard, the Theatre, Qinfang Pavilion and Daoxiang Village.

Also by the Dianshan Lake, the Fork International Rafting Club is a more expensive tourist place. Occupying an area of nearly 11 hectares, the club includes KTV facilities, a sauna, beach volleyball grounds, swimming pools and restaurants serving both Chinese and Western food. The best facilities of all, however, are the 50 classy five-person water-skiing leisure boats. Since a club membership costs US$10,000, the club is described as the "ivory tower" of the consumer world of Shanghai.

For visitors with a particular interest in ancient Chinese bridges, Jinze Town not far from the lake is a must. On an area of half a square kilometre, the town has 21 bridges. Interestingly, all the bridges here have temples and all the temples are built with bridges.

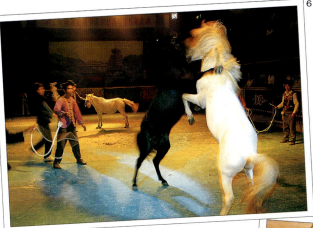

Jiading's Confucius Temple and Dragon Pool

Winding up a trip to Dianshan Lake, visitors might go further north and after 40 kilometres will arrive at Jiading, the most northwestern town of Shanghai. Already a town during the Zhou Dynasty, it grew into a county during the Qin period from 221 to 207 B.C. Of the many sites of historical interest still preserved to this day are the Guyi Garden, Autumn Glow Garden, Confucius Temple, Nanxiang Brick Pagoda, and so on.

In Jiading District, a recent tourist addition is the Liuhe Island Folk Custom Holiday Village. Surrounded on three sides by the ancient Liuhe River, the island is slightly more than 76 hectares in size, with orchards, pastures and children's camping sites. Visitors can rent a boat to drift on the river, go fishing or be guests at farmers' homes, where they can see how farmers fluff cotton, spin cloth on a wooden loom operated by hand or try doing things unusual to urban life, such as how to pedal a waterwheel, walk on stilts and push a wheelbarrow.

A Bird's-Eye View Tour

Those visitors who are in Shanghai on return trips will not fail to notice the physical changes that have taken place in Shanghai in the past few years. These changes have offered new ways to tour Shanghai. The new high-rises, including not only buildings but also bridges and the TV tower, now offer the visitor panoramic views of the city. For those in a hurry, half a day will be fine. If you have just finished seeing the old Shanghai town, you are pretty near the Nanpu Bridge, which is the third largest cable-braced bridge in the world. One end of the bridge is near the Sanshan Guild Hall. The elevator at the bridge end takes the visitor to the pedestrian walkway on the bridge. This advantageous point offers a nice view of both Pudong and Puxi or districts on both banks of the Huangpu River. Coming down from the bridge, the visitor is advised to take a taxi for time's sake, though many buses have their terminuses at the end of the bridge. Crossing the bridge to the east bank, the South Pudong Road leads to Lujiazui, on whose ground stands the towering Pearl of the Orient — the TV tower which, at a height of 468 metres, is the tallest building in Asia. Though not yet fully open to the public, this bird's-eye view of Shanghai is soon to be a tourist attraction. From here, going along the Pudong Avenue, one comes to Yangpu Bridge which is the largest cable-braced bridge in the world. Like the Nanpu Bridge, elevators here take visitors to the bridge's surface. One may choose to take a quick look at the bridge by driving in a car, although no stopping is allowed on the bridge. Then, at the west end of the bridge, which joints with the Inner Circle Road, one can move onto the north-south Tibet Road to go to the People's Square. Recently rebuilt, the large park like square is home to the Civic Tower, the new Shanghai Museum, Shanghai Theatre, a large-size music fountain and an underground shopping mall. A quick look at the square may be completed in half an hour, but it takes at least half a day to see the museum and do some shopping. The newly completed subway in Shanghai is aimed at easing Shanghai's communications. Naturally the People's Square is the site of one of the stops. Thus, visitors may go and get a ride on the subway train to Xujiahui Square and take a look at the new face of the district, or to the Gubei District to see how real estate business is booming as large groups of villa houses are going up and being sold, or get off at the stop at Huaihai Road to see how people in Shanghai do their shopping.

These tourist routes suggested so far cannot include all the tourist attractions in Shanghai. The following are some of the places that visitors can go.

A Nightclub

After 8:00 p.m., one can go and enjoy a performance by a traditional jazz band at the Peace Hotel. If you want to see a nightclub where residents in Shanghai have fun, the 70-year-old Great World is a must. At the crossing of East Yan'an and Xizang roads, the Great World features folk variety shows on the first floor, different kinds of operas, such as the Hu opera, Yue opera, Peking opera, Kunqu opera, Wuxi opera and Huai opera or farce shows, magic shows, acrobatics, or other local art shows alternating on the second floor. The third floor is where people come and play games and bowling and on the fourth floor there is a conservatory, a dance hall, a coffee shop and a music teahouse.

When hungry, folk delicacies particular to Shanghai should not be missed. Places to go include three "food streets". The Yunnan Road is full of small food stands operating from early evening till late at night. The Zhapu Road north of the Suzhou River is known for well-built restaurants which operate all day and night and where food is naturally a little expensive. Huanghe Road is somewhere between the two.

Translated by Huang Youyi

Treasure-Hunting in Shanghai

TEXT BY ER DONGQIANG

If you want to seek for the past, or if you are an enthusiast of antiques and the curious, it's worthwhile to stay in Shanghai for a couple of days.

Antique collection is very popular in Shanghai. Recently, many antiques collectors have started roving and routing here, searching for valuables in stalls scattered along streets and lanes. Some places are well-established while some are new. We introduce the best among them in the following brief guide.

Flea Markets

Zhonghua Xin Road: These are all private trader with fixed stalls. They are open all day, selling antiques. hardware, electrical appliances, bicycle parts, etc. Though the largest market in Shanghai, it mainly handles everyday items. But there is always the possibility that something special may be found among the bric-a-brac.

Dongtai Antique Market: There are about 200 stalls, operated by private traders. They are open all day and sell antique ceramic, stone, padauk and gold ornaments. They also sell flowers, birds, fish and insects such as crickets. Staff from Shanghai's foreign embassies are known to frequent this market. Owners of Shanghai's large antique stores also visit the market to augment their stock.

Liuhe Road Antiques Market: Located near Dongtai Road with a width of 45m and more than 100m in length, there are over 150 stalls selling antiques and handicrafts with an estimated 10,000 bargains and curios such as stationery, calligraphy and paintings, baskets, embroideries, jade ware, ivory carvings, painted porcelain, bronze bowls, tin basins, padauk furniture, teapots and so forth. Some store owners also sell and collect souvenirs of the Cultural Revolution such as photos and armbands. This antiques street has over RMB 10 million yuan in sales volume each year.

Fuyou Road Antiques Market: Open only on Sundays, there are over 800 mobile stalls. It is the largest antiques market and well-known in Shanghai for its high quality and range of goods. In order to occupy a good location every Sunday, many hawkers and stall owners gather before dawn to bring their wares and treasures. Needless to say, the price of transactions is relatively high and there is a tendency for dealers to talk in the market jargon. Be ready to haggle: this authentically and literally unpriced, and priceless, hotchpotch of stalls is ideal for mavens from home and abroad.

Zhaojiabin Old Coins and Stamp Collecting Market: Located at the junction of Zhaojiabin and Taiyuan Road in West District, this market specialises in old coins and stamp exchange. Buy, sell or part exchange: it attracts many amateur and overseas collectors.

Antique Stores

Shanghai Antiques and Curios Store (194-226 Guangdong Road); Antiques and Curios Branch of Shanghai Friend-ship Store (1000 Yan'an Road Central); Antique Section of Shanghai Friendship Store (33 Zhongshan No. One Road East): These three are the oldest antique shops in Shanghai and together offer the best and most complete range of antiques in the City. Unlike the flea markets, they mainly cater for overseas visitors.

Weixin Antique Store: It is situated at Jinling Road East and is Shanghai's largest shop selling antique clocks and watches from China as well as of (foreign-made). Most of its best timepieces were once owned by wealthy people in old Shanghai.

Xiequn Antique Store: At the junction of Nanjing and Fujian roads, this is an old store selling optical instruments, antique clocks and watches, padauk furniture, electrical appliances, etc.

Chuangxin Antique Store: At the junction of Huaihai and Changshu roads, it used to be called Jinmen (Golden Gate) and was quite famous in the 50s. It sells quality leather goods, clocks and watches, and ornaments.

Shaanxi Antique Store: At the junction of Shaanxi West and Yan'an roads, it caters mainly for foreign customers and sells porcelain ornaments, antique clocks and watches, and artefacts.

Xinguang Optical Instrument Store: At the junction of Huaihai Central and Yandang roads, this is also an old shop (Formerly called Wanjing), in fact the city's most famous shop specialising in both old and new optical instruments and secondhand cameras. Its staff are also among the very few people in Shanghai who can repair old cameras. It sold only modern products for a while after changing its name to the present Xinguang, but recently resumed dealing in old and antique optical instruments.

Xiangsheng Trading and Trust Store: No.173, Shaanxi Road South near Huaihai Road, specialises in various kinds of old clocks, watches and cameras. Many actors and actresses from Hong Kong and Taiwan come here to hunt for items.

Hua Bao Lou: Located in the newly-renovated basement of the City God Temple, this is Shanghai's largest indoor market for a wide assortment of goods. Choose from over 200 large and medium sized counters selling painted porcelain, jade ware, lacquerware, calligraphy and paintings, rubbings, embroideries, carvings, etc.

Enjoy yourself with the arts, sightseeing and shopping. This prosperous Shanghai Old City God Temple has reappeared in full swing.

Shanghai's Family Museums and Exhibition Houses

- **Shanghai Folk Collection Exhibition House**
  (1551 Zhongshan Road South)
- **Bao Wanrong Theatrical Costumes Exhibition**
  (No. 11, Lane 138, Rushan Road, Pudong)
- **Chen Baocai's Butterfly Exhibition**
  (No. 2, Lane 77, Zichang Road, Pudong)
- **Chen Baoding Calculation Instruments Exhibition**
  (No. 8, Lane 378, Jianguo Road West)
- **Chen Yutang's Collection of Ancient Jars**
  (326 Xizang Road South)
- **Du Baojun's Collection of Rain Flower Stones**
  (No. 268, Caoyang Village 5)
- **Fang Binghai Family Collection of Ancient Cases**
  (F/3, No. 4, Building 10, Honglu Sub-area)
- **Huang Guodong's Collection of Paper Fan Coverings**
  (No.1, Lane 47, Ninghe Road, Nanshi District)
- **Hu Renfu's Collection of Root Sculptures**
  (No.13, Lane 470, Loushanguan Road)
- **Peng Tianmin's Collection of Natural Models**
  (No. 23, Lane 60, Linyin Road)
- **Xu Binjie's Collection of Boat Models**
  (No. 131, Lane 1143, East Yuhang Road)
- **Huang Genbao's Collection of Miniature Musical Instruments**
  (No. 6, Lane 41, Daling Road and Pailou Road)
- **Wang Xianbao's Collection of Nine Dragon Fans**
  (No. 1125, Wayu Matou Street)
- **Wei Zhi'an's Museum of Agates**
  (No.6, Lane 21, Balin Road)
- **Xu Sihai's House of Tea Art**
  (No. 332 Xingguo Road)
- **Yu Liuliang's Numismatic Collection**
  (267 Hongzhen Laojie)
- **Zheng Genhai's Collection of Rare Shells**
  (No. 42, Laoshan Village 2, Pudong)
- **Zhao Jinzhi's Museum of Golden Keys**
  (11 Xueye Road, Pudong)

Major Scenic Spots

Scenic Spot	Address	Opening Hours	Briefing
The Bund	Zhongshan Road East 1		Well-known both in China and overseas for its Western classical buildings, the bund is virtually an "international architectural exhibition".
Shanghai Yuyuan Garden	132 Anren Road	8:30-17:00	The largest classical garden in Shanghai. with the famous the "Exquisite Jade" and unique shopping area of traditional temple style
Jade Buddha Temple	170 Anyuan Road	8:00-12:00 13:00-17:00	Wood carved Buddha idols, Buddhist scriptures, two jade Buddhas
Longhua Temple / Pagoda	2853 Longhua Road	7:00-16:00	A traditional temple and pagoda with ancient Buddhist scriptures. In the third month of the lunar calendar every year, a temple fair is held.
Lu Xun's Memorial Hall / Tomb	146 Jiangwan Road East (Inside Lu Xun Park)	Park: 5:00-22:00 Memorial Hall: 8:30-11:30, 13:30-16:00	The tomb of Lu Xun is a granite construction built in Shaoxing style. Original manuscipts, and literature by Lun Xun; photos of Lun Xun, and his bronze statue
Yangpu Bridge Nanpu Bridge	Huangpu River	Yangpu: 8:30-16:00 Nanpu: 8:30-16:30 (Jan.-May, Oct.-Dec.) 8:30-22:00 (June-Sept.)	7658m in length, Yangpu Bridge spans 602m across the Huangpu River and ranks first in the world of its type.
Site of The First National Congress of the Communist Party of China	76 Xingye Road	8:30-11:00, 13:00-16:00 (Closed on Mon., Thu.)	Birthplace of the Chinese Communist Party; the first National Congress was held in July 1971.
Dr. Sun Yat-sen's Former Residence	7 Xiangshan Road	9:30-11:00, 14:00-16:30	Residence of Dr. Sun and his wife, Madame Soong, from 1919 to 1924
Madame Soong Ching Ling's Former Residence	1843 Huaihai Road Central	9:00-11:00, 13:00-16:30	1948-1963 work place and residence of Madame Soong: Exhibits include books and articles left by Madame Soong.
Shanghai Municipal Children's Palace	64 Yan'an Road West	9:00-11:30 (Opened on Wed., Sat.)	Shanghai's largest comprehensive outdoor educational and activity institution for children; a grand celebration on June 1 each year
Shanghai Arts & Crafts Research Institute	79 Fenyang Road	8:30-16:30	Research institute for embroidery, carving and handicrafts.
Confucius Temple	183 Nanda Road, Jiading District	8:00-11:00 13:30-17:00	Built in 1219, the attached examination hall where visitors can study the Imperial Examination System
Huilong Pool Park	299 Tacheng Road, Jiading District	7:30-16:30	Built in the Qing Dynasty; a magnificent stage with fine carvings
Autumn Glow Garden	314 Dongda Road, Jiading district	8:00-16:30	Also known as "City Garden", a privately-owned garden built in the Ming Dynasty with elegant scenes of four seasons.
Guyi Garden	Dehua Road, Nanxiang Town, Jiading District	6:00-16:30	Built in the Ming Dynasty. With many historical relics, including a stone pillar inscribed with Buddhist scriptures, and a pagoda
Jinjiang Paradise	At the junction of Humin and Hongmei roads		Large amusement park with motor-driven games
Shanghai Zoo	Hongqiao Road, Changning District		One of the largest zoos in China, with over 340 species of rare birds and animals both local and from abroad.
Chuansha Park, Heming Tower	ChuanshanTown, Pudong New District		A traditional style garden covering an area of about 1.7 hectares. Heming Tower is a 7-storey 54m-high tower.
Dianshan Lake Tourist Area	Located West of Zhujiajiao Town, Qingpu County	8:00-16:30	Two scenic spots with Water Sports World, youth camp base and golf course
Shanghai Grand View Garden	Jinze, Qingpu County	8:00-16:30	Based on a description from the Chinese classical novel A Dream of Red Mansions, an ancient style garden with beautiful scenic spots.
Qushui Garden	Northeast of Qingpu County	8:00-16:30	Built in the Qing Dynasty with many plants over a hundred years old and various styles of ancient architectures
Square Pagoda/Screen Wall	235 Zhongshan Road Central, Songjiang County Town, (Inside Square Pagoda Park)	6:00-17:00	Built in the Northern Song Dynasty, it is a brick pagoda with vivid and delicate carvings in the style of the Tang Dynasty.
Zuibai Pond	64, Renmin Road South, Songjiang County Town	8:00-16:30	Located in the Sheshan Scenic Area. On the peak of Sheshan Mountain there is an observatory and the largest cathedral in the Far East.
Exhibition of Shanghai Popular Collections	1551 Zhongshan Road South	9:00-16:00 (Closed on Mon.)	More than 200 catagories of folk collection.
Sihai Teapot Museum	322 Xingguo Road	9:00-16:30	Established by collector Xu Sihai, more than 1000 types of folk collection such as purple clay teasets and painted porcelain, the largest teaset can serve 600 people.

Administrative Organizations Related to Foreign Affairs

Name	Address	Telephone	Fax.	Post Code
Shanghai Municipal Tourism Administration	2525 Zhongshan Road West, Huating Guest House	4391818x2309	4391519	200030
China Chamber of International Commerce, Shanghai Chamber of Commerce, China Council for the Promotion of International Trade, Shanghai Sub-Council	14/F, New Town Mansion, 55 Loushanguan Road	2750700	2756364	200335
Division of Aliens and Exit. Entry Administration of the Shanghai Municipal Public Security Bureau	210 Hankou Road	3723030x20706		200002
Foreign Affairs Office of the Shanghai Municipal People's Government	1418 Nanjing Road West	2565900		200040
General Administration of Customs of the People's Republic of China, Shanghai Branch	13 Zhongshan Road East 1	3232410		200002
Office of Overseas Chinese Affairs of the Shanghai Municipal People's Government	913 Huashan Road	4317126 / 4317143	4314026	200031
Office of Taiwan Affairs of the Shanghai Municipal People's Government	54 Lingyuan Road	2758877	2756961	200335
Shanghai Foreign Economic Relations and Trade Commission	New Town Mansion, 55 Loushanguan Road	2752200		200335
Shanghai Foreign Investment Commission	New Town Mansion, 55 Loushanguan Road	2752200		200335
Shanghai Frontier Defence Inspection Station of the People's Republic of China	81 Dianchi Road	3213199		200002

Major Travel Agencies

	Name	Address	Telephone	Fax	Post Code
Category A	Shanghai Tourist Corporation	2 Jinling Road	3217200	3291949	200002
	China Comfort Travel Service, Shanghai Branch	15/F, Tower 1, Chang'an Building 1001 Chang'an Road	3174249 / 3178705	3174751	200070
	China Merchants International Travel Shanghai Co.	277 Wuxing Road	4727534 / 4722682	4726992	200030
	Huating Overseas Tourist Corporation	4/F, Shanghai Hotel, 505 Wulumuqi Road North	2480088x4007 / 2485469	2485470	200040
	Oriental International Travel & Transport Corp. Ltd.	549 Shaanxi Road North	2476228	2470585	200040
	Shanghai China International Travel Service	2 Jinling Road	3217200 / 3234202	3291788	200002
	Shanghai China Travel Service	881 Yan'an Road Central	2478888 / 2475878	2475521	200040
	Shanghai Crane International Tours Inc.	85 Xianxia Road	2333998	2331308	200031
	Shanghai CYST Tours Corp.	2 Hengshan Road	4331826 / 4330151	4330507	200031
	Shanghai Great World International Travel Service	220 Xizang Road Central	3204468 / 3204293	3224210	200002
	Shanghai Jinjiang Tours Ltd.	27/F, 100 Yan'an Road East	3262910 / 3290690	3200595 / 3230360	200002
	Shanghai Spring International Travel Service	1558 Dingxi Road	2520000	2528795	200050
	Shanghai Workers' International Travel Service	1/1017 Hongqiao Road	2193500	3243282	200051
	Shanghai Donghu Travel Company Ltd.	Room 204, Ruijin Building, 205 Maoming Road South	4720631 / 4736844	4729338	200020
	Shanghai International Good Will Travels	Room 301, Office Building, International Equatorial Hotel, 65 Yan'an Road West	2483091 / 2482507	2483773	200040
	Shanghai New Asia International Travel Corporation	69 Xizang Road Central	3523568	3276534	200003
	Shanghai Railway Administration International Travel Service	East Building, Shanghai Railway Station, 203 Moling Road	3179234x3219	3177312	200070
	Shanghai Yangzi Tourism & Trading Co.	Room 58641, Building 3, Jinjiang Club, 58 Maoming Road South	2582582x58641 / 4721272	4721466	200020
Category B	China Changjiang Cruise Overseas Travel Corp. Shanghai Branch	56 Sinan Road	4721970 / 4728239	4726438	200020 / 200001
	China Golden Bridge Travel Service Co. Shanghai Branch	Lantian Hotel, 2400 Siping Road	5485344 / 5485906	5485344	200433
	East Shanghai International Travel & Trade Corporation	580 Pudong Avenue	8841527x57	8861546	200120
	Shanghai Hengshan International Travel Company	Room 21, Hengshan Hotel, 534 Hengshan Road	4373050 / 4715429	4715429	200030
	Shanghai International Culture Travel Company	19/F Xin Min Wan Pao Bldg., 839 Yan'an Road Central	2475636	4729306	200040
	Shanghai Peace International Tourism Corporation	639 Huashan Road	2484458 / 2489009	2481898	200040
	Shanghai Radio & TV International Tourism Company	2 Beijing Road East	3218177 / 3290137	3290087	200002
	Shanghai Women's International Travel Service	245 Tianping Road	4371536 / 4330001	4371336	200030

Major Recreational Centres

Name	Address	Telephone
Grand Cinema	216 Nanjing Road West	3273399
Cathay Cinema	870 Huaihai Road Central	4373757
Metropolis Cinema	500 Xizang Road Central	3226624
Shanghai Film Art Centre	160 Xinhua Road	2400668/2400992
Changjiang Theatre	21 Huanghe Road	3279531
China Theatre	704 Niuzhuang Road	3517839
Yifu Cinema	701 Fuzhou Road	2336270/3225487
Dawutai Theatre	663 Jiujiang Road	3224509
Lanxin Theatre	57 Maoming Road South	2530788
Shanghai People's Art Theatre	284 Anfu Road	4330069
Shanghai Acrobatic Theatre	400 Nanjing Road West	3274958
Shanghai Concert Hall	523 Yan'an Road East	3183197
Cassablanca KTV Disco	30/F Rainbow Hotel 2000 Yan'an Road West	2753388
City Club	26/F City Hotel 5-7 Shaanxi Road South	2551133
Galaxy Recreation Centre	2/F, 35/F Galaxy Hotel 888 Zhongshan Road West	2752999/2755888
Melody Bar	Yantze New World Hotel 2099 Yan'an Road West	2750000
Limelight Karaoke	Hotel Sofitel Hyland 505 Nanjing Road East	3515888
Midnight Star	Holiday Inn Yin Xing Shanghai 388 Panyu Road	2528888
Paradise Disco	Jianguo Hotel 439 Caoxi Road North	4399299
Club Le Carman	5/F Shanghai Orient Shopping Centre 8 Caoxi Road North	4071818
Club Top Ten	8/F Portman Shangri-La Hotel 1376 Nanjing Road West	2798638
Gordon Blue International	8/F International Shopping Centre 527 Huaihai Road Central	3589999
Jinjiang New Century Night Club	59 Maoming Road South	2582582/4317312
New Town Club	35 Loushanguan Road	2757888/2753793
Shanghai International Seamen's Club	60 Huangpu Road, 2/F 3 Zhongshan Road East 1	3251500/3218060
Golderen Night Club	2088 Yan'an Road West	2757667
Seven-skies Club	651 Nanjing Road West	2585237
Shanghai Venus Recreation Club	301 Huashan Road	2488888
Shanghai Stadium	111 Caoxi Road North	4385200
Shanghai Natatorium	1500 Zhongshan Road South 2	4385200
Shanghai Diving Pool	1380 Fuxing Road Cenral	4710237
Jing An Tennis Court	468 Wulumuqi Road North	2525199
Xuhui Tennis Court	85 Hengshan Road	4710622
Shanghai Pudong Shooting & Amusement Co., Ltd.	Binhai Township East, Nanhui County	8196765
Shanghai International Golf Country Club Ltd.	Zhujiajiao, Qingpu County	9728111
Shanghai FECC International Yacht Club Co., Ltd.	Sales Department: 1453 Yan'an Road West	2520222/2523567
Great World Entertainment Centre	1 Xizang Road South	3263760
Jinjiang Amusement Garden	Humin Road, Hongmei Road South	4364956
Shanghai Art Gallery	456 Nanjing Road West	3272684
Shanghai Library	325 Nanjing Road West	3273176
Shanghai Old Jazz Band	1/F Peace Hotel, 20 Nanjing Road East	3211244
Hotel Drama "The Grand and Brilliance in a Culture of 5000 years"	Jiaqing Hall, Rainbow Hotel, 2000 Yan'an Road West	2753388x3318 (not regularly performed)
Huangpu River Cruise	229 Zhongshan Road East 2	Embark: Jan.-May, Nov.-Dec. 14:00 June-Oct. 9:30, 14:00, 19:00
Wang Yi Ji Art Tea House	28-38 Jinling Road	3276155

Star-Rated Hotels

Name	Star-Rated	Address	Telephone	From Airport (km)	From Railway Station (km)	Fax	Post Code
Garden Hotel Shanghai	5	58 Maoming Road South	4331111	14	4	4338866	200020
Jinjiang Tower	5	161 Changle Road	4334488	14	4	4333265	200020
Portman Shangri-La Hotel	5	1376 Nanjing Road West	2798888	14	3	2798999	200040
Shanghai Hilton International	5	250 Huashan Road	2480000	12	4	2483848	200040
Shanghai JC Mandarin	5	1225 Nanjing Road West	2791888	14	3	2791822	200040
Sheraton Hua Ting Hotel Shanghai	5	1200 Caoxi Road North	4391000	10	10	4390232	200030
Tai Ping Yang Westin Hotel	5	5 Zunyi Road South	2758888	6.8	8	2755420	200335
Galaxy Hotel	4	888 Zhongshan Road West	2755888	6.8	8	2750201	200051
Holiday Inn Yin Xing Shanshai	4	388 Panyu Road	2528888	9	7	2528545	200052
Hotel Nikko Longbai Shanghai	4	2451 Hongqiao Road	2559111	1	10	2559333	200335
Hotel Sofitel Hyland Shanghai	4	505 Nanjing Road East	3205888	17	4	3204088	200001
Jianguo Hotel Shanghai	4	439 Caoxi Road North	4399299	11	8	4399433	200030
Jinjiang Hotel	4	59 Maoming Road South	2582582	14	4	4725588	200020
Peace Hotel	4	20 Nanjing Road East	3211244	18	5	3290300	200002
Rainbow Hotel	4	2000 Yan'an Road West	2753388	6.8	8	2757244	200051
Shanghai International Equatorial Hotel	4	65 Yan'an Road West	2481688	12	4	2481773	200040
Shanghai Lansheng Hotel	4	1000 Quyang Road	5428000	25	8	5448400	200437
Yangtze New World Hotel	4	2099 Yan'an Road West	2750000	6.8	8	2750750	200335
City Hotel Shanghai	3	5-7 Shaanxi Road South	2551133	10	10	2550211	200020
Hengshan Hotel	3	534 Hengshan Road	4377050	9	8	4335732	200030
Huating Guest House	3	2525 Zhongshan Road West	4391818	14	4	4390322	200030
Jing An Hotel	3	370 Huashan Road	2481888	12	4	2482657	200040
Jinjiang Pacific Hotel	3	104 Nanjing Road West	3276226	15	3	3999620	200003
Longmen Hotel	3	777 Hengfeng Road	3170000	14	Adjacent to railway station	3172004	200070
Magnolia Hotel	3	1251 Siping Road	5456888	22	8	5459499	200092
Ocean Hotel Shanghai	3	1171 East Daming Road	5458888	23	5	5458993	200082
Park Hotel	3	170 Nanjing Road West	3275225	15	3	3276958	200003
Shanghai Hotel	3	505 Wulumuqi Road North	2480088	12	4	2481056	200040
Shanghai Mansions	3	20 Suzhou Road North	3246260	18	5	3999778	200080
Haigang Hotel	2	89 Taixing Road	2553553	14	3	2550151	200041
Nanjing Hotel	2	200 Shanxi Road South	3221455	17	4	3206520	200001
Wugong Hotel	2	431 Fuzhou Road	3260303	15	4	3282820	200001
Yangtze Hotel	2	740 Hankou Road	3225375	16	3	3206974	200001

Climatic Conditions in Shanghai

Description \ Month	Jan.	Feb.	Mar.	April	May	June	July	Aug.	Sept.	Oct.	Nov.	Dec.
Average Temperature (°C)	3.5	4.6	8.3	14.0	18.8	23.3	27.8	27.7	23.6	18.0	12.3	6.2
Average Highest Temperature (°C)	7.6	8.7	12.6	18.5	23.2	27.3	31.8	31.6	27.4	22.4	16.8	10.7
Average Lowest Temperature (°C)	0.3	1.4	4.9	10.4	15.3	20.1	24.7	24.7	20.5	14.3	8.6	2.7
Rainfall (mm)	44.0	62.6	78.1	106.7	122.9	158.9	134.2	126.0	150.5	50.1	48.8	40.9

Major Restaurants

Name	Address	Telephone	Specialities
Sun Ya Restaurant	719 Nanjing Road East	3207788	Cantonese Fried shrimps, saute sliced chicken and beef, fried crisp skinned chicken, roast suckling pig
Xijiaoting Seafood Restaurant	1333 Nanjing Road West	2790279	Cantonese, seafood Seafood showered with cashew nuts, baked crab, steamed shrimps, steamed eel
Lishui Restaurant	68 Lishui Road	3265947	Cantonese and Sichuan "Qian Long Banquet"
Yanyunlou Restaurant	755 Nanjing Road East	3226174	Beijing Braised shark's fin, braised bear's paw in "four treasure", Beijing roast duck, edible bird's nest
Meilongzhen Restaurant	22, Lane 1081, Nanjing Road West	2535353	Sichuan food Fried prawns in chili sauce, wheat flour cakes with pork sliced, mandarin fish in chili sauce with noodle, gingko eggplant with shrimp meat
Green Willow Village Restaurant	763 Nanjing Road West	2538427	Sichuan and Yangzhou Fried crisp duck, salted jelly-like pork, fried beef with orange peel, fried shredded fish
Yangzhou Restaurant	308 Nanjing Road East	3225826	Huaiyang Salted jelly-like pork, steamed crab meat balls, Mos' beancurd shred, mashed fish with pinenuts
Old Town Restaurant (Lao Fan Dian)	242 Fuyou Road	3289850	Shanghai Eight delicacies in pungent bean paste, braised fish, fried crab, sweet soft-shelled turtle
Wanbaohe Restaurant	603 Fuzhou Road	3207609	Crab feast "Delicate Chrysanthemum Pattern Crab Cuisine"
Gongdelin Vegetarian Restaurant	43 Huanghe Road	3270218	Vegetarian Saute "crab meat", fried shredded "eel", scrambled egg with dried mushroom, fried "fish" slices with green peas
Xiaoshaoxing Restaurant	75 Yunnan Road South	3281826	Shaoxing Delicious tender boiled chicken and chicken porridge
Hui Feng Lou	89 Henan Road South	3281795	Muslim Braised ox legs, steamed mutton, Hui style mutton, sliced chicken breast
Lübolang Restaurant	131 Yuyuan Road	3280602	Shanghai and Taihu Lake dim sum Steamed bun with mushroom and vegetable fillings, soft cakes with "three shreds", "zongzi" dumplings, mashed dates crisp cake
Kawakyu (23/F Shanghai Hotel)	505 Wulumuqi Road North	2481836	Japanese Sushi, hotpot, set menus and banquets
Kampachi (4/F Hotel Equatorial Shanghai)	65 Yan'an Road West	2481688	Japanese Sashimi, Sushi, Teppan Yaki, broiled dishes,
Shiki (2/F Portman Shangri-La Hotel)	1376 Nanjing Road West	2798888	Japanese Sushi and Teppan Yaki
Benkya Restaurant (2/F Hotel Nikko Longbai)	2451 Hongqiao Road	2559111	Japanese Tempura, set menus
Sakura Restaurant (2/F Garden Hotel Shanghai)	58 Maoming Road South	4333111	Japanese Snow course
Ginza Japanese Restaurant (Jinjiang Hotel Compound)	59 Maoming Road South	2582582	Japanese Barbecue, barbecue assorted dishes, steamed rice
Belvedere (1/F Hotel Equatorial Shanghai)	65 Yan'an Road West	2481688	European Continental Banana flambe, fried king prawns with butter grating, stewed rabbit in red wine sauce, American grilled beef
Shanghai Jax (1/F Portman Shangri-La Hotel)	1376 Nanjing Road West	2798888	American and European grill Jax signature pizza, Jax beef from grill, jax special flavour
Bund European (3/F Jinjiang Tower)	161 Changle Road	4334488	Luxurious French restaurant
Shanghai Rainbow Seoul Restaurant (1/F Rainbow Hotel)	2000 Yan'an Road West	2753388	Korean Materials and cooking machinery are import from Korea and the food is prepared by a famous Korean chef.
The Dreamland Cafe Spice Garden (1/F Yangtze New World Hotel)	2099 Yan'an Road West	2750000	Southeast Asian buffet

Major Shopping Centres

Name	Commodities	Address	Telephone
China Tourist Souvenir Corporation	Handicraft articles, antique imitations, souvenirs from other places	1000 Yan'an Road Central	2790279/2472180
Chinese Ancient Bookstore	Ancient books, calligraphy and paintings, stationery, handicraft articles	424 Fuzhou Road	3224984/3207745
Duo Yun Xuan Art Studio	Calligraphy and paintings, stationery, rubbings, seal cutting	422 Nanjing Road East	3223410/3223939
Jukai Enterprise Co., Ltd.	Jewels, gold and silver ornaments, handicraft articles	1376 Nanjing Road West	2798335
Shanghai Antique and Curio Store	Porcelain, jadeware, ornaments, ed sandalwood furniture, embroideries, paintings, seals and inkstones	218-226 Guangdong Road	3214697/3213559
Shanghai Arts and Crafts Import and Export Corporation Sales Department	Jewels and ornaments, red sandalwood furniture, embroideries, stationery, paintings and handicraft articles	817 East Daming Road	5463066/5454919
Shanghai Arts and Crafts Sales Service Centre	Jadeware, ivory carvings, jewels, gold and silver ornaments, embroideries, screens, leather goods, stationery and carpets	190 Nanjing Road West	3275299/3276530
Shanghai Arts and Crafts Trading Co.	Handicraft articles, medicine and garments	1000 Yan'an Road Central	2790279x2111/2474781
Shanghai No.1 Food Store	Sugar, tea, farm produce, game from land, cigarettes, wine	720 Nanjing Road East	3222777
Shanghai Foreign Languages Bookstore	Foreign books, maps, cassettes, CDs, handicraft articles	390 Fuzhou Road	3223200
Shanghai Foreign Trade Emporium	Handicraft articles, daily necessities, garments, cosmetics and medicine	24 Nanjing Road East	3230148/3230174
Shanghai Friendship Store	Food, garments, stationery and handicraft articles	40 Beijing Road East	3294600
Shanghai Goodwill Shop	Handicraft articles, souvenirs, stationery and medicine	1700 Beijing Road West	2584213/2550500x104
Shanghai Hualian Commercial Building	Daily articles	635 Nanjing Road East	3224466
Shanghai Jing De Zhen Porcelain Art Ware Sercice Dept.	Porcelain and handicraft articles	1175 Nanjing Road West	2530885/2533178
Shanghai Lyceum Jewelry and Antique Store	Jewels, porcelain, paintings, ivory, seals, antiques	A 398 Changle Road	2551667/2538459
Shanghai No. 1 Department Store	Daily necessities, garments, handicraft articles and stationery	830 Nanjing Road East	3223344
Tong Han Chun Tang Traditional Chinese Medicine Store	Chinese herbal and patent medicines, Western medical instruments	20 New Yuyuan Road	3731232/3285230
Manhattan Plaza	Daily articles, garments	463-477 Nanjing Road East	3222239
Mosta Commercial Building	Daily articles, garments and ornaments	889 Nanjing Road West	2175076/2566992
Shanghai Huating Isetan Co.	Daily articles, famous brand garments, gifts and ornaments	527 Huaihai Road Central	3751111
Shanghai International Shopping Centre	Daily articles	527 Huaihai Road Central	3750000
Hongxiang Dept. Store (Burberrys)	Daily articles, famous brand garments, gifts and ornaments	869 Nanjing Road West	2582688
Lao Zhou Hu Cheng Chinese Writing Brush & Inkstick Store	Writing brush and inkslabs, stationery	90 Henan Road Central	3214488
Quan Guo Native Products & Specialties Food Store	Native products and food	491 Huaihai Road Central	3721466/3720775
Shanghai No.2 Food Store		955 Huaihai Road Central	4730777/4730666
Shao Wan Sheng Groceries		414 Nanjing Road East	3223907
Golden Hawk Famous Brand City	Various kinds of famous brand articles	889-909 Huaihai Road Central	4732828/4739398
Shanghai No.1 Yaohan Department Store	Famous brand daily articles	577-587 Nanjing Road West	2567009x11
Crocodile International	Garments	328-332 Shaanxi Road South	3277459
Esprit	Ditto	224-230 Huaihai Road Central	3281531
Giordano (Jing An Hotel)	Ditto	425 Wulumuqi Road North	4387420
Itokin	Ditto	335 Henan Road Central	3226280
Jeanswest International	Ditto	114 Nanjing Road East	3213730
Mexx (Hongxiang Dept. Store)	Ditto	869 Nanjing Road West	2582688
Montage	Ditto	360 Xizang Road Central	3223083
Mysheros	Ditto	309 Shimen Road (1)	2153258
Nike	Ditto	400 Huaihai Road Central	3270876
Pepsi		829 Nanjing Road East	3222560
Pierre Cardin	Leather goods and handbags	338 Huashan Road	2483272
Playboyl(Huating Isetan Co., Ltd.)	Garments	527 Huaihai Road Central	3751111
Puma	Sports wear	1000 Huaihai Road Central	4731721
Valentine (Huating Isetan Co., Ltd.)	Garments	527 Huaihai Road Central	
Cai Tong De Drugstore	Rare medicinal herbs	320 Nanjing Road East	3207418
Shanghai Chinese Medicine Trade Centre	Ditto	506 Henan Road Central	3251990/3214174
Shanghai No.1 Dispensary	Ditto	616 Nanjing Road East	3224567
Watson's Personal Care Store	Cosmetics, daily articles and personal care	1376 Nanjing Road West	2798382
Shanghai Shui Hing Dept. Store	Daily articles	152 Huaihai Road Central	4722944
Shanghai Sunrise Dept. Store	Ditto	718 Caoxi Road North	4387420
Shanghai Women's Store	Women's articles	447 Huaihai Road Central	3721595
Kintetsu Department Store	Daily articles	1376 Nanjing Road West	2789376

Major Transportation Companies

Name	Address	Telephone	Fax
Air France, Shanghai Office	Room 32223, International Arrival & Departure Building, Shanghai Hongqiao Airport	2558817	
China Eastern Airlines, Shanghai Booking Office	200 Yan'an Road West	2475953 (Local) 2472455 (Int'l)	2476761
Dragon Air Hongkong, Shanghai Booking Office	Room 123-125, North Building, Jinjiang Hotel	4724852/4723671	4728174
Japan Airlines, Shanghai Office	Room 201, Ruijin Building	4336337	4336450
Korean Airlines, Shanghai Office	Room 104, Shanghai International Equatorial Hotel	2481555/2557555	2481666/2557666
Northwest Airlines, Shanghai Office	2/F, East Tower, Shanghai Centre	2798088	2798007
Russian Airlines, Shanghai Office	70 Donghu Road, New Wing of Donghu Hotel	4331020x77401	
Shanghai Airlines Booking Office	555 Yan'an Road Central	2551551/2550550	2550251
Shanghai China International Travel Service, Hongqiao Airport Office	Hongqiao Airport	2428474/2558899x5462	
Shanghai China Travel Service, Hongqiao Airport Office	Hongqiao Airport	2558899x5464/2428335	
Singapore Airlines Ltd., Shanghai Office	Room 208, Office Building of Shanghai Centre	2798000/2558703	2798027/2798028
Southwestern Airlines, Shanghai Booking Office	150 Maoming Road South	4333355	4711676
United Airlines, Shanghai Office	250 Huashan Road	2553333	
Xinjiang Airlines, Shanghai Booking Office	370 Changde Road	2474497	2474496
Shanghai China International Travel Service, Shanghai Railway Station Office	Shanghai Railway Station	3179168/3172441	
Shanghai China Travel Service, Shanghai Railway Station Office	Shanghai Railway Station	3179251/3179327	
Shanghai Railway Station Inquiry Service	Shanghai Railway Station	3179090	
Shanghai Tourist Taxi Co.	16 Wuzhong Road	4383420/4383564	4381113
CYTS, Shanghai Taxi Service Co.	1300 Zhongshan Road South 2	4381824/4382372	
Shanghai Dazhong Taxi Shareholding Co. Ltd.	16/F, 920 Nanjing Road West	3207207/2585033	
Shanghai Donghu Taxi Service Co.	30 Donghu Road	4710265/4336086	4710265
Shanghai Friendship Taxi Service Corporation	847 Yan'an Road Central	2791279/2584584	
Shanghai Hengshan Taxi Service Co.	70-80 Yiminsha Road	5446060	
Shanghai Shihua Taxi Service Company	Weier Road, Jinshanwei (Inside Shihua Automobile Transportation Co.)	7932975/7932000	7942245
Shanghai Taxi Corporation	920 Nanjing Road West	2151515	2151160
Shanghai Xinhuaihai Taxi General Co.	630 Bansongyuan Road	3762618/3770101x2513, 2613	
Shanghai Zhenhua Taxi Corporation	150 Lingyuan Road	4391188/2758800	
China Ocean Ship Agent Co., Shanghai Co.	13 Zhongshan Road East 1	3290088	
Shanghai Ocean Shipping Company	378 East Daming Road	5416200/5192888	5458984
Shanghai Port Passengers General Terminal, Inquiry Office	1 Jinling Road East	3261261	
Shanghai Port Passengers General Terminal, International Passengers	1 Taiping Street, East Daming Road	5419529	
Shanghai Ocean Shipping Tally Co.	3 Liyang Road	5461583	

Consultants: Wang Nai Li, Dao Shuming
Compilers: Shanghai Municipal Tourism Administration
              Hong Kong China Tourism Press
Planner: Wang Miao
Executive Editors: Chan Yat Nin, Tu Nai Hsien
English Editor: Kuang Wen Dong
Art Designer: Ling Kwok Po
Publication Supervisor: Lai Chung For

Published by Hong Kong China Tourism Press
ISBN 962-7799-19-X
First Edition, First Published February 1995
All rights reserved. No parts of this book may be
reproduced in any form without permission of the publisher.